NOT WITHOUT TEARS

Not
Without
Tears

BY HELEN CALDWELL DAY

SHEED AND WARD • NEW YORK

1954

This book is dedicated to my mother and to Dorothy Day, because without their help and encouragement it could not have been written at all; in fact, the story wouldn't even have been.

The names of some of the people in this book are fictitious, as is the name of St. Bridget's Church. Some incidents have also been slightly altered to disguise the identity of the people involved.

NOT WITHOUT TEARS

1

Blessed Martin House was started in answer to a need, the need of people for love and understanding and material assistance given in such a way that it does no violence to their dignity as children of God, called, as it were, to share the life of God, to be co-heirs with Christ, as St. Paul says. The house actually opened in 1951, but long before that it existed as an idea in my own mind, formed according to the pattern of St. Joseph's House of Hospitality of the Catholic Worker, in New York City, where I had worked as a volunteer. St. Joseph's House had been started by Dorothy Day, a convert to Catholicism from Communism, and Peter Maurin, a Frenchman, having as its general aim to "realize in the individual and in society the expressed and implied teachings of Christ, beginning with an analysis of our present society, to determine whether we already have an order that meets with the requirements of justice and charity of Christ."

I first came in contact with the Catholic Worker movement in 1947, through my friend Father Meenan, who had been my instructor when I became a convert to the Catholic faith. I was eighteen, and a student nurse at the Harlem Hospital School of Nursing. I was not then much impressed by what I saw at the Catholic Worker, mostly because of the poverty of it and its disorder. I did not like poverty in any sense. I had grown up in it, hating it and wanting to escape from it into renown and success. My father was a teacher in a little Southern college, and his salary had always been small; often my mother had had to work in order that we might have a barely comfortable living, or something just short of this. But here were a group of people, many little older than myself, who took the counsel "Blessed are the poor" seriously and were voluntarily living a life of poverty with the poorest in the slums of New York off the Bowery. They ate and worked and prayed and shared their house with people I had always thought of as just "bums." And they seemed to be happy doing it, though all were obviously capable of doing something "better."

I did not like their ideas about poverty. But I did like what they said about race, about us all being one in Christ. Since I am a Negro myself it grieves me unutterably to see so many of my own people buried in the sordidness, the drabness and the ugliness of city slums and small-town ghettoes as the result of intolerance and hate—discrimination and segregation—and I long to have a share in the resurrection which must come, and find it easy to love and respect those others I meet, of whatever race or creed, who share that same desire.

So I worked as a volunteer at the Catholic Worker for about a year, and gradually, as I worked, I began to change my ideas on a lot of things—things like poverty and "bums." I began to see what Peter Maurin meant when he called the poor "ambassadors of God." A retreat with a small group and Father Meenan's brother completed the metamorphosis, and instead of being scandalized by the Worker, I now felt myself more and more drawn to become a part of it.

I could see that good was being done. The poor were being fed and clothed and sheltered through the personal sacrifices of the members of the staff. Race seemed to matter not at all, and ordinary people like myself were living and working together in order to grow in grace and in love of God in each other, and in love of the Church, her liturgy and sacraments.

The thing that still held me back, even after I had become inwardly convinced that this was the life I wanted to live, was concern for my son, McDonald Francis, or Butch, as we call him. He was then about a year old. His father and I were no longer together and there was no hope of a reconciliation. Since my husband was in the Navy then, we were getting an allotment, but once he was back in civilian life I knew that we could expect little help from him. I would be our main support, and I wondered whether I had the right to impose this life on my son: could I deliberately choose poverty when I had a child?

Then in the fall of 1948 I became ill with tuberculosis and had to go into a sanatorium. At the same time Butch was crippled by polio and had to go to a hospital for several months. While we were both sick, I had a lot of time to think, and I found myself adopting new values and new ways of looking at things. Butch was home, almost fully recovered, long before I was, and by the time I was discharged from the sanatorium I had reached a decision about many things. It seemed to me that the things Butch would gain by the experience of growing up in the house I envisioned would outweigh anything he might lose by it.

And I now saw clearly that we are in the hands of God anyway, and that many worse misfortunes than poverty—our illnesses, for instance—could befall us no matter how hard I tried to "plan" our lives together. I saw Tamar, Dorothy Day's daughter, who had grown up in such a house of hospitality, and I asked no more of God than this: that Butch should grow up as well-adjusted, friendly, and full of charity.

I had been in the sanatorium in New York, but after my discharge I came to Memphis, where Butch was living with my mother and my stepfather. I had decided to find a job in Memphis as soon as the doctor said it was all right, and to start my house of hospitality there, or in some nearby town or city. I wanted to work in the South because I knew the need there, and because so often Negroes whose talents and training would enable them to do something to alleviate the suffering of Negroes in the South refuse to stay there; they go North where they can live and work with some semblance of peace and security. I do not blame them in the least; on the contrary, I sympathize with their problem; it is one I have had myself. It is hard to go back to the South if you have ever lived away from it, when you are a Negro. Even now, four years after my own return to the South from New York, it means a real and painful effort, every time I return again after a journey North. As soon as the "White Only," "Colored Only" signs begin to appear, something inside me shrinks and I feel choked and hurt. But still I come back

I decided on Memphis or a nearby town so that Mother and I could still be close to help each other. Besides, it is easier to start where you are known, and where you know the problems.

When I had been in Memphis about six months I met

a young white man about my own age who was also a Catholic and full of real apostolic zeal. We found that we had much in common, and became friends and talked of starting an interracial group of people interested in Catholic Action, who would study, work, and pray together. We wanted to study the social teachings of the Church in the light of our own problems and needs, as well as learn more about the Church herself, her liturgy and sacraments. We knew that it would not be easy to start a group like this and keep it going. Even before we started there were difficulties, mostly with our own families.

Jim's father was not at all sympathetic to his ideas on the racial question, or on capital and labor, or on a lot of like problems. Since Jim lived in his father's house and depended on him for support, that created a serious problem.

In my own family, my mother was wholly in sympathy with my ideas and plans and helped me to develop them. (My parents are divorced, but since my mother was my father's second wife and the first is living, her marriage to him was invalid in the eyes of the Church; thus, although divorced and remarried, she was able to become a Catholic. She became a convert the year after I entered the Church.) My father was living about forty-six miles from us, but I saw him often and found him always ready to listen to anything that interested me. There is not in him a trace of racial hatred, so far as I have ever been able to see, and he encouraged the formation of the group.

However, my stepfather, who is also very dear to me and was at that time the main support of Butch and me, was very like Jim's father with regard to race. He doesn't like Negroes very much (though he is one), but he likes white people even less and feels that none of them can have a love for, but only a desire to use, the Negro. He did not say I might not have my friends in the house, but he did predict all sorts of trouble because of it. He was afraid the neighbors would complain to the police and we would be charged with running a disorderly house. He was sure that my racial ideas were going to get me into trouble one way or another.

"You just can't mix the races," he kept insisting one evening when we got into one of our arguments. "You were never intended to. But no, you're bull-headed like your mother. No one can tell you anything. You think a man named Jesus the Jews made up a long time ago can save you. But this is a white man's country. You-all don't like to admit it, but I'm not one to try to fool myself. I know where I stand. You can have all your meetings and your fathers and popes and preachings, but you aren't going to change that. A white man is a white man and a zigaboo is never going to stand with him. He was made for a servant, and that's what he'll always be."

"What does that make you, then?" I said.

"Oh, I don't like it, but it fits me too. I know it, though, and you-all don't. You won't admit it for yourselves."

"We can't admit what is not true. Sure, God made us different, like He made the grass and the flowers and the trees different. But they all drink the same rain and put their roots in the same earth, and the tree doesn't say to the flower, 'This is my puddle.' You talk about Negro and white, but I notice you like good food, and a warm house and decent clothes. You want your shirt ironed and your socks clean." I looked around the comfortable house as I talked. His eyes followed my gaze.

We were then living in the housing project where Mother and Don still live. There are gas, electric lights,

6

running water, an electric refrigerator, and a washing machine. In the kitchen there are cabinets for dishes and foodstuffs, attractive though inexpensive table and chairs, and a gleaming linoleum on the floor. In the front room are comfortable chairs, a couch, and little tables strewn with knickknacks. Mother has embroidered pretty scarves for the furniture, and there is a bright rug on the floor. The room is lighted by several lamps; from the shining floor to the pictures on the walls, it reflects comfort and cheer.

"You see," I said, "*you* want to be free to do the work you like and live in peace. Nobody else, 'zigaboo' or white, wants anything more than that, and the right to love God as they believe."

"No," he retorted, "that's the zig who wants that. Any white man who isn't a fool knows better. You are the only ones going around with your hands folded looking up to heaven for help from a man who couldn't even save himself from the cross. Everyone else is looking out for the good American dollar. All your preachings and meetings and discussions don't carry as much weight as that!"

Then we really started to argue; "All your money," I said, "won't ever carry as much weight as the love some men have for God and each other. That is what has kept the Church He founded going for two thousand years, even if He didn't come down from the cross to suit you and others like you." (I couldn't resist adding this last.)

"He didn't because he couldn't. He was just a man. The Jews told him to come down and they would believe. And he didn't because he couldn't."

"So you say the same thing, though He did an even greater miracle?"

"What miracle?"

7

"His resurrection."

"There was no resurrection. That's just a fairy tale. When you're dead, you're dead, and there is no resurrection. You've seen what happens to things that die, they smell. They don't rise, they rot. When you zigs get that through your heads, maybe more of you will have that warm house, and food and things you were talking about. As long as you stay buried in this fairy tale about Jesus you'll always live in alleys and jump when a white man whistles. You'll always be the tail-ends and get the leavings."

"Funny, it's those who believe strongest in this 'fairy tale,' as you want to call it, who are doing the most to get people out of squalor and despair and bring them hope, and a chance to live like people instead of cattle."

"That's what the priests tell you."

"They don't have to tell me. I can see for myself. I'm not blind. Besides, it stands to reason it would be so. If—*if*, I say—a man really believes, as you say you believe, that he is the center of his own universe, and that all the things he does and wants revolve around himself, then he wants to get as much as he possibly can for himself. And that means that someone else is going to get left out. It means the strong man is bound to take away the weaker man's rights. But if—and again I say if—a man truly believes in God and loves Him and tries to imitate Him—giving, giving, giving as much as he can of himself and his love and his goods— then someone is going to benefit. And, incidentally, the man who gives won't lose out either; the more he gives, the more he will receive."

"You talk like a fool." He said it with a smile intended to soften it, but he meant it.

"In your eyes, from your point of view, I guess I am.

But it is because Jim and the others like him, and I and others like me, believe as we do, that we can forget about race and come together and work and study to improve ourselves so we can help others improve themselves and the conditions around them and around us all."

He made a mocking sound. "Forget! Don't ever imagine a white man forgets he's white or forgets your're black, and you'll save yourself some tears."

"Father Meenan said to me once that there is only one remedy for evil, and this is grace, but grace is bought by sanctity and sanctity by suffering. So I don't mind the tears. I'd rather shed them."

"I thought your mother was bad enough, but I can see you are *both* crazy. All right, then. Go on, be bull-headed. Stick your neck out. But when you get in trouble, don't come bellyaching to me. You're just like a Nigger I saw down on Beale Street one day. He came out of Red Johnny's and the cops got him for something. He kept arguing with them, and they told him to shut up or they'd knock him in the head. He was bull-headed like you, though. 'You mean you gonna hit me?', he said, 'on my haid!' " (And Don's imitation of words and expression was, I was sure, perfect.)

"The cops told him again to shut up and come on if he didn't want them to knock him in the head. He stopped, took off his hat, and said again, 'You mean you gonna hit this haid?' That cop hit him in the name of the law! And he was decent. If it had been me, I'd have split his damn skull. He was asking for it. And you are asking for it. Whatever you think, or I think, there's a law here, and it separates white from colored, and it means for you to stay on your side of the fence and the other fellow to stay on his. That way there won't be any trouble."

9

"I'm not afraid of trouble, if I have to go against my conscience to avoid it," I said. "Jim and I want to start a group to study and work together. It's going to be a Catholic group; that means faith and good-will will be the criteria of membership, not race nor anything else like it."

"No, what you want to do is mix the races up. Look, take this glass of water and that milk. You mix them together and what have you got? Neither water nor milk. But *you* think *you'll* have milk. You can't get what *you* want. You'll get nothing if you try."

"It all depends on what you were trying to get in the first place."

"Well, I'm not saying the other fellow's crazy. Maybe it's me. But here's the way it is, see, as I see it. I want a break now because it's me. But if I were on the other side of the fence, I'd make damn sure I'd stay there, one way or another. That is what they've done, that's the English system. If you don't give the other guy a chance, he can't beat you. It's a poor gambler who gives the other fellow loaded dice."

"And it's a crook who uses them himself."

"Look, I've been a gambler, and I don't play it that way in a good game. But I want the odds on my side. If we've got to play with a loaded pair, I want them to be mine."

Arguments like this usually took place at the table right after dinner, since that was about the only time during the week that Don and I were home together, except Sundays. The children, my son Butch and my nephew Lawrence, would listen in wide-eyed silence. Often Mother and I would talk about it afterwards, and we both feared the effect of Don's attitudes on the children, because they loved him so much. For that reason, one or the other of us would frequently cut the discussion short. And we tried doubly hard, too, by our own words and examples, to make up for his lack of faith, making it seem—as it was—a joyful thing to attend Mass together and have prayers together at home, that they might glimpse some of the delights of faith in God's love. I was glad when Jim or his friends were especially kind to them, because this more than anything Mother or I could do or say gave the lie to what Don said about race. The best proof there is that there can be love between the races is love shown between members of the different races.

But despite our difficulties with family and friends, and with finding a priest who could moderate such a group, we didn't lose interest but kept trying. One priest we approached said he was interested but just too busy, and sent us to another. Then he telephoned the latter, said we were dangerous radicals and advised him to have nothing at all to do with us. Another priest who heard us out was afraid to get involved in anything interracial. He was no longer young, and once in Memphis he had been made to suffer a great humiliation on Beale Street because of his interest in the Negro problem. Another was suspicious of lay Catholic Action in general. And some simply weren't interested at that time in the kind of group we proposed.

That was our strength and weakness, I suppose, that the group should be so flexible. The qualifications for membership were broad. A member might be white or colored, Catholic or non-Catholic, so long as he was interested in the life of the Church as the Mystical Body of Christ and the welfare of the members therein. Jim's special interest was in the intellectuals; I only hoped to find people full of love and a desire to give themselves to the work and study.

One thing that we insisted upon was that race itself

11

should not be stressed directly, but that instead we would bring it in as naturally as possible, as a part of the other social problems or a cause of them, together with other causes and other problems. We did this because the racial problem is more than a problem of color. It is a problem of housing, of wages, of work, of families, of many different things. If some of these problems are solved, much of the "racial problem" will be solved. We wanted to be inter-racial as the Church is interracial, because the truth is too big for any one people. And because Christ is in all and loves all.

We had many difficulties before we found a priest with the vision, courage, and time combined, to serve as moderator of the group. But at last one, Father Coyne, a Josephite, agreed to help us. The Josephites are a religious order of priests who work among the Negroes. They take a special vow for this work, and all the ones I've met have shown a genuine interest in their adopted people. Father Coyne certainly did, and his parishioners all loved him. We were very glad when he agreed to help us.

We had the same difficulties finding members. People were too busy, or they were afraid, or they simply weren't interested. But at last we had a small group of white and colored people who were enthusiastic and looked forward to our first meeting.

For us that first meeting was monumental. Not that we accomplished a great deal, we did not. But it was something real, a new beginning. The conception of a new life in the Church in Memphis. Here for the first time, as far as we or anyone we knew could tell, a group, albeit a very very small group of Catholics, white and black, representing the fairly secure middle class and the poor and insecure, had come together, not in answer to urgent necessity, not just to work together in some public work of mercy (the war had accomplished that, as need always does, need and common suffering) but simply out of love for God. I think all felt the call to action and to a love that leaped the bounds of race and embraced all men, but the first love was the necessary one, the love of God for Himself, a love that could make our enemies our brothers.

For here we are enemies, the white and the black and brown. And it is very hard for us, no matter which side we are on, to see, beneath the color of the skin, the face of Christ, loving us and imploring our love in return. Christ in us—Christ in all men—it's hard to believe in the doctrine of the Mystical Body sometimes, when we have grown up in the loneliness of hatred and suspicion, distrust and prejudice. In times of distress, here as everywhere, often men for men's sake sense this basic relationship and forget, to a great extent, the great barrier of color; and men are men, and not colored or white. Yet always in the background, like a monster lurking ready to pounce, is the demon of prejudice, waiting for one to step over the faint line that is still there and forget one's place, so that this unity, good as it is, is not enough.

That is why we rejoiced in the knowledge that it was the love of God that had drawn us together, and the desire to learn to love each other in Him. I think few of us could really have deceived ourselves so early with the belief that our love was already perfect, and color forgotten completely; but all of us wanted that love because Our Lord said "A new commandment I give you, that you love one another as I have loved you" and we wanted not to forget color, but to have it not matter. It was the love of Christ that brought us together and that could keep us together if only we could grow in that love. And how we wanted to do that!

We met at the rectory of St. Anthony's Church. Father Coyne helped us to make coffee and set out the cups. This was one of many practices we had borrowed from the Catholic Worker and Friendship House. Coffee was to be the ice-breaker, a mark of friendliness that was intended to put all at ease. To us it was a little more too, though none of us put it into words for a long time. It was a mark of equality and brotherhood, because down here white people do not eat and drink with Negroes. It is one of those strange twists of prejudice. We may stand together in an elevator, nose to nose, or in a pinch sit together on a bus or train. We may wait in the same line for something we both want, or work together on the same job, but we don't eat or drink together.

So it was fitting that we, who ate one Bread, should break more common bread together, that we who dined together at the table of the Lord should sup together. The coffee and rolls, so little in themselves, bridged chasms, as a mark of our sincerity. It was a sort of test, a measure by which we could see who belonged. Some who would have come if there had been only a lecture or a discussion would not come where there was eating and drinking. They wanted to be charitable, but at a distance.

"I agree with the Catholic Worker in some things," one woman told Jim, "but not on the racial question. They don't understand us down here."

So many white people believed that one could be just without being charitable, or that one could be charitable without being tolerant. So many said things like: "The Negro is all right in his place, but would you want your

sister to marry a Negro?" To them, coffee and rolls together would inevitably lead to that, and that was the
intolerable evil.

On the other side, the Negroes were more evasive.
They did not give that as an excuse but said they were
"too busy," they would "surely come down sometimes,
but . . ." Yet I often knew the real reason. Sometimes they
told me or told my mother that they were afraid and
unwilling to get "mixed up" in anything interracial: "It's
no use looking for trouble. You are used to being with
white people, but I wouldn't be comfortable. I wouldn't
know what to say. Maybe sometimes I will come. . . ."

". . . You go ahead. They can be so friendly to your
face, but behind your back . . . I don't know. I guess I'll
just stick to my own color."

So it had been hard on both sides, finding members of
the group, hard for Jim and for me, and I don't suppose
that either of us could guess just how difficult it was for
the other. We each wanted to reach members of the other's
race with this philosophy of love and Christian revolution,
a philosophy which, Peter Maurin said, was "old, so old
that it looked like new"—but we especially, I think, wanted
to reach our own. It is only natural to love first our own,
those bound to us by ties of blood or belief or common
suffering. And to a certain extent this is good, and even
necessary.

It is in its abuse that it becomes evil, when its inner
meaning is perverted. "Love your neighbor," Our Lord
said; that is, the people next door, the people we can help,
the people who share in some way our lives, first; not the
far-off people of Timbuctoo, who can share only in the
heroic actions of our dreams and benefit by the greatness
of our imaginations. Surely we can have no real love for

the people of remote countries if we have none for those we see every day. St. John put it another way: "If a man boasts of loving God, while he hates his own brother, he is a liar. He has seen his brother, and has no love for him; what love can he have for the God he has never seen?" What love, indeed? And how can he love God, Christ, in the people of other races when he cannot see Christ in the people of his own? So we loved our own, and because we loved our own, we loved the other.

At the first meeting we got acquainted; we exchanged ideas; we tried to explain ourselves: "We are a group of lay Catholics come together to study and practice the truths of our Faith. Any person, whether Catholic or not, interested in attending the meetings, is welcome as long as he understands and agrees that we are discussing social problems in the light of Catholic teaching. We shall not deal with apologetics. We shall assume that people present accept the basic truths of the Church.

"Our program, in the beginning at least, is to be one of study and discussion in order that we can have a sound basis for action. The action, when it comes, is to be, as it were, a spilling over of our inner life, of our prayer life. It would be good if we all got a copy of Dom Chautard's *Soul of the Apostolate*. That will give us a real idea of what we are trying to accomplish. From this group, eventually, we hope there will come forth leaders who will do something about Catholic Action in Memphis."

The question was asked, "Shall we seek episcopal approval? And after the discussion we decided that we should, but not yet, not until we had something more concrete to present to the Bishop. The idea of an interracial lay group in the South was too new.

Finally we closed with a prayer. Then some went

16

home, but most stayed to help wash the dishes and put them away, and straighten up the kitchen. As we worked, we still talked. Already we felt we had accomplished something, we had met together, eaten together, and now we were working together, with no trace of selfconsciousness or unpleasantness. We had broken the ice, at least, that froze the two races apart, and that made us happy.

2

At home, mother was as enthusiastic as I over the success of our beginning. She liked my new friends and tried to make them feel welcome whenever they came. We had little, but of that she shared gladly, giving me coffee and cookies, or money to buy other refreshments for our meetings (for I had not gone back to work yet and had no money of my own).

Don was still not reconciled, but when I had company, he was polite as always. Only mother and I, knowing him, could feel the strain behind the politeness, and felt keenly for him, wishing he would change, knowing that his hate hurt him really as much as it did us. It is a terrible thing not to believe in God or in His grace in people. It is a terrible thing to hate.

Butch was perfectly happy. He liked Jim and Dot and all the others and took them as casually for granted as he did his other friends. He was only four and he hadn't learned what prejudice is. I didn't want him to learn it for himself. I wanted him to learn love; to learn to like people for Christ's sake, and for their own sakes; not for the way they looked or talked or dressed or the color of their skins. More than I cared to admit, I feared what the South can do to a colored boy, crushing his spirit, aborting his manhood, so that he is only half a man—the other half dead, murdered along the way by those white people who "don't have anything against Negroes, but . . ." and those colored who "don't say the white man is much better, but a nigger just ain't no good, just like a fly, everything he touches he lights on, and that's what spoils it."

I didn't want him to think the world was all sweetness and light. But I did want him to know—as Don and so many others of my acquaintance didn't seem to know—that those things are there too. There is suffering, loneliness, poverty and insecurity in the world; in his four years, he had already discovered something of that in his months in the hospital with polio. But there is love too, and the richness of the security of being loved, and there is joy. And every child needs those things too. They are the armor and weapons he uses to fight against the harsher things. They make a gate in his heart to God's love, because you can tell him about the love of God who loves and is loved. He can believe. That is grace building on nature, as is its wont.

I was glad then that he continued to have friends of both races, so he could form, in these early and impressionable years, a truer idea of differences—and not only he, but all his friends too. He will meet prejudice some day— in fact he already has, now that he is in school and must ride the buses, which are segregated—but how much easier it will be for him to see in these things the actions of persons and not race; or if he sees race, it is with definite reservations. That is enough to build upon.

I tried to explain this to my colored friends, Ruby and Dave, who I hoped would be interested in joining the study group. Ruby agreed with me, with a "but." Dave was not so sure. "Maybe you are right," he said, "but I wouldn't want Nay" (his son) "to marry a white girl, and I guess they feel the same way. I don't like them any better than they like me. Maybe not as well. All I want is for them to let me alone and give me a chance too. I don't want to live in their houses or go to their shows or send Nay to their schools; but I want houses and shows and schools as good."

Rosemary and Morris, our other special friends in the neighborhood (also colored), understood better. They were both interested in the study group, and Morris, or Rose's eldest daughter, Evelyn, would baby-sit while Rose came to the meetings. But then, we were always doing things together—taking our children on outings in the country to fish and play, helping each other with the work at home, going to church together and planning little surprises for our children together.

Then there was Mr. Childs, another colored friend, who was blind. He was, with me, a member of the Catholic Union of the Sick,[1] so he understood something of the meaning of suffering, sacrifice and poverty as means to good. He was often inarticulate, but he believed firmly in the unity of men in God and in our obligation to help in the restoration of all things to, and in, Christ. He loved the study group and attended every meeting, except when someone forgot to call for him. Such forgetfulness seldom occurred.

---

[1] The Catholic Union of the Sick is an international organization headed in the United States by Mrs. Robert Brunner, which is made up of small groups of the physically handicapped or ill who offer their prayers, sufferings and sacrifices for specified and general intentions for the good of all. The group is usually referred to as "Cusa," and its members as "Cusans," in the United States.

Then there was Richard, another neighbor and friend who often drove me to the colored parish church in his car. He liked to argue about the things we discussed in the group meetings, but he would never attend one himself. He was suspicious and distrustful of the lay apostolate, especially in any form that remotely resembled or suggested that of the Catholic Worker, which he disliked, or Friendship House, which he distrusted. I think that was because he had such a high regard for his friend Father Joe, who had no use for these groups nor any like them; in fact he was suspicious of lay Catholic Action in general, and Richard looked at us through Father Joe's eyes. Richard often came to visit me, and we argued about race and the Church, about the Mass and liturgical prayer, about education and economics, all sorts of things. He was, in almost everything, extremely conservative, and, strangely, always on the defensive.

Another colored friend, Charlene Marshall, whom I had met at church because she also attended Mass daily (which is very unusual in our church) was soon interested in the study group. She spoke little but thought clearly and logically. She was quite fervent, and I really hoped that perhaps it was she who would some day be interested in helping me to open a house of hospitality in Memphis. But hers was a more perfect call, and she entered a religious order the next year. Until that time, however, she worked and studied well with the group.

There were a few other colored people who came to our discussions occasionally, but at this time, these were the only ones who came regularly enough for all of us to get to know them. There was Lester, who once or twice gave a party in his home for us, and Lillian, Rosemary's sister, and Jessie, another friend of mine. Later Gladys

Kinkle started coming, and when she did, she was a conscientious member.

There were more white members. Some were friends of Jim and some were those whose names we had got from the Catholic Worker as people who might be interested in the kind of program we proposed. There were three girl scout leaders. Two of them were not Catholics at the time the group was started. However, by the end of the year both had started taking instructions, and eventually they were baptized. They had come into the group because of their interest in social and economic problems such as race and wages and housing and jobs. And when they learned that the Church has an answer for these as well as for problems of the spirit, they were convinced of her divine mission.

There was another non-Catholic, Ted Williams, who was a teacher in one of the white colleges. He was a very brilliant man and had also come into the group through his liberal views on various social problems. Later he, too, became a convert, but that was yet far away, so far as we could then see.

There was another white member who remained in the group only a short time. He was the only member that I ever saw openly discourteous to colored members, apparently out of prejudice but possibly out of blind stupidity. For instance, after the meetings when small groups gathered for conversation, if he were in a group that included colored people, he invariably ignored their presence and talked around and over them of things and people unknown to them. If they ventured a comment, he seemed annoyed, and once or twice I saw him ignore the comment. I was glad when he left.

Then there was Jack, who seemed friendly enough to

all but who was greatly preoccupied with his own personal problems and had little time to give to the group. He was also a little afraid of the possible social complications that could arise from memberships in an interracial group.

There was Bill, another recent convert like myself—young, friendly, and perhaps the best-liked by the colored members. He was full of the kind of energy and zeal that just need a push in the right direction to produce tremendous effects. He went into the Army before the question of establishing Blessed Martin House came up. But he brought many new members into the group first, and among these were some of the best friends Blessed Martin House was to have in the group. Linda John was one of these. She was the mother of five children, and very busy, but she often found time to come to our discussions. I will say much more about her later.

There were other housewives and mothers too, Alice Hanrahan and her husband, Eugenia and her husband, both couples deeply interested in the group. Sometimes both husband and wife attended, but most of the time it was just the wife.

There were several students, Joan, Sarah, Sue, Gerry, and Martha. Occasionally there were others as well. They were readers of many of the magazines concerned with the Christian revival, such as *Today* and *Integrity*, and books like von Hildebrand's *Transformation in Christ*, Goodier's *Church, Growth or Decline?* They knew a little about people like Dorothy Day, the Baroness de Hueck (who started Friendship House), Jacques Maritain, and Eric Gill.

They were feeling their way through a new, and to them strange, world, and it was hard and frightening. It was a world of faith most of their parents had not known and did not want them to know, and it was always a struggle to reconcile the demands of their faith with their duties to and love for their families. They lived in an environment that was hostile to the teachings of Christ when they touched upon the social order, an environment which would have pushed Him, too, into a place in the background where He would be silently and unobtrusively worshiped.

Then there was Jim. He was a natural leader, and the supernatural gifts of wisdom, prudence, knowledge and understanding superimposed on these natural qualities by his Confirmation had been effective in making him a better one. "The Christian conscience" was a favorite expression of his, and he had it, in regard to race, to poverty, to family life, to all these problems we discussed.

I did not always agree with him, but I admired and respected him. And most of our disagreement was on method and approach rather than spirit and idea. Basically we were at one. Perhaps really our differences were simply the exaggerated differences of the qualities that make men and women complements to each other rather than equals, as if they were the same and could be measured by the same measure. He was one of the most objective persons I have ever known. He was unemotional too—I don't know that I've ever seen him angry, or really emotionally disturbed by anything. And his approach was chiefly through the intellect—and to the intellectual.

I am more subjective, and tend to feel things keenly even as I know them. I tend to become one with the thing or person that has my attention, so much so that it is difficult for me to regard them objectively, so my approach is more one of the will. God will enlighten our intellect even without our cooperation, if our ignorance is a hindrance to the work He wants us to do. That is not the usual way, perhaps, for He expects us to search for and find truth; still He will show us Himself even when we don't want to see Him.

But He will never force our wills. He will never ravish, but only woo. He will make us know and understand, but He will not make us love.

So my approach is one of love. I would reach the head through the heart to move the will. Jim would reach the heart through the head to move the will. But we both would act from the same motive.

He was markedly unselfconscious and "natural" in his spirituality. If he wanted to share his gifts of the mind, one had to admit there was plenty there to share. Everything, even the most difficult subject, seemed to become so simple to him. And I liked to listen to him.

In planning the meetings for the study group or talking about its final aim, a favorite expression of his was "group dynamics." "The idea of group dynamics, of community cooperation," he would say, "is that all submit themselves beforehand to the will of the group, not that they compromise pragmatically where they have to. It means that, in making a decision, some should present the evidence, reserving their judgment. Then the group should begin to discuss the pros and cons of it, examining as a group the various facets of the evidence. If there is general agreement when all thoughts are out, this is it. If there is not general agreement, the alternatives are, first, to consider something else, or, if it is necessary to choose immediately, to come to a vote, looking at the vote not quantitatively but qualitatively; that is, if it is not decisive on the part of those whose judgments are most to be respected, another alternative should be sought. In this sense there is no compromise."

I agreed with him in this, as much as I understood it, but it seemed to me that such group dynamics could only be employed in a very well-knit community where the people concerned truly shared the same problems and aims, a family, a community of people living together, or working together daily on the same job, as in a factory; a group of students in a school or some such basic community. I did not believe a group as varied as our study group could employ such dynamics in the fullest sense, because I did not believe that all, even most, would or could submit themselves beforehand to "the will of the group" in the sense that they must in a different kind of community. I believed, though, that we should have our group work toward this sort of dynamics.

Again, in discussing the purpose of the group, we were discussing some members, and he said, "I'm afraid that some of the members' concentration on the Church is too wholly involved with the Church's solution to the social question —labor and race particularly. We must try to impress upon them what the Church is, that it is more than a means to a social reform. The Church is the instrument of worship, the means of glorifying God, first by prayer, second by virtue in the soul, third by virtuous action. But action, as far as the Church is concerned, is a part of Christianity only insofar as it flows from and to worship and personal and community virtues. For instance, pure utilitarianism would bring a community to racial justice and economic justice if the community saw what would be best for itself, seeing it purely on the selfish and biological plane. But the Church does these things in the name of God and for the glory of God and for its own sanctification. I have spent many evenings talking capitalism, racism, and fascism with them, hoping and trying to turn these things to their ultimate ends. We are concerned with the social problem, but we must be more concerned with worship in society and virtue in society. We must be careful not to regard these things back to front."

I agreed with him fully in this, and he had expressed, better than I ever could, a very real difficulty we were constantly coming against in the group. If we could have pushed God and Church into the background, we could have won many "liberals," white and colored, as new members of the discussion group. But our interest in the social questions existed because of our Faith, not despite it, as many seemed to believe.

Another thing Jim and I frequently discussed between ourselves, though seldom at the meetings, was the question of the Catholic Pacifist. He was of the opinion that the position was theologically untenable. I was in the very opposite position. We were always reading more about it, each bringing the results of our reading to the other's attention. We neither reached an agreement in this nor changed each other, but we kept each other thinking, and alive to the fact that the Church permits different views on this, as in many other matters, and we could each respect the other's conscience in the matter.

We never, or almost never, talked race between ourselves. There seemed to be no need. He was frank about the prejudices of some other members of his family and deplored them, even while he understood them. But, to my knowledge, the only concessions he made to them were: (1) he never asked us to his home to have our meetings, as some of the other members of the group did, except for one special occasion; (2) when he wrote anything in our local paper about race or capitalism, he used a pen name; and (3) he expressed unwillingness to give out *The Catholic Worker* and *The Interracialist* at the church his family and his family's friends attended (although he would give them out elsewhere). And we respected these courtesies he did his parents. We never questioned his own sincerity or lack of prejudice because of his family's attitude.

One thing we freqeuntly talked about was community. "I am for a community of men who love one another, and love one another chiefly because they know one another," he said.

My own idea of community was not quite the same. "I am for a community of people who love one another chiefly because they love God and recognize Him in each other," I answered, trying to explain. "To know each other, in my experience, is not necessarily to love each other, except in God. But to know He is there in the other makes it possible for us to love even the unlovely and unlovable, to love the stranger and the friend—or rather, to make the stranger also a friend."

But he lived up to his idea of community, and in the study group sacrificed many of his ideas, hopes, and ambitions to the will of the group, embryonic community that it was. He was convinced that in this is the source of Christian restoration. And it was to this that he had dedicated himself.

As I learned to know him better, I hoped more and more that he would find in the lay apostolate his own vocation. I especially hoped that he would want to join me in starting a house of hospitality modeled after the

Catholic Worker house in principle, but fitted to our own needs. As time passed, however, this seemed more and more doubtful. For one thing, he did not agree with much that was a part of the Catholic Worker movement, and for another, he was most interested in teaching. He wanted a world that dealt more with the intellect than with physical activity. He seemed to have nothing against manual work; it just didn't seem to strike him as important.

Besides this, he was being constantly pushed on all sides, by his friends, his confessor and, I think, some members of his family, to consider a vocation to the priesthood. I knew, and he knew, that his father, who opposed his ideas on the Church and society as a layman and was a little ashamed for him, would have taken a certain pride in having him a priest, even with those ideas. Or perhaps, to be more accurate, his father supposed or hoped that the seminary training would crush these "radical ideals" out of existence.

So most of the summer he spent trying to decide between a teaching career and the trial of a vocation. He was so much interested in teaching that he did not want to be a priest unless he could also teach (at least, this I gathered from our conversations). He was convinced that he could do the most good teaching but was afraid he ought to try a vocation to the priesthood, because that is more perfect in itself. He thought he could resolve his difficulty by combining the two.

There were a few others in the group who came now and then: two nurses from the Catholic hospital, two teachers from the public schools, and a young lawyer who loved to argue, preferably against whatever Jim or I suggested for the good of the group. The variety made for interest if not for unity, and our discussions were thought-provoking if at times a little heated. But I think they were always charitable.

Sometimes we tried to plan things to do together, like Mass attendance in a body and Communion breakfasts. But some were afraid, and then there were difficulties in finding pastors who were willing to permit an interracial group to meet at their churches for Communion breakfasts. We said Compline, the official night prayer of the Church, together in English at all our meetings, though, and sometimes went together to Benediction of the Blessed Sacrament at St. Anthony's Church with Father Coyne.

A lot of people wondered how we stayed together; few had expected the group to persevere, but we did. Supernaturally, it was grace that held us together; on the natural plane, it was Jim's personality. He was a born leader. And he had a real interest in the group and faith in the accomplishment of its purpose.

3

THE STUDY GROUP WAS ALMOST A YEAR OLD WHEN THE doctor told me in July that I could go back to work but would have to continue taking pneumo-thorax treatments (a procedure for the collapse of the lung often employed in tuberculosis). I was very happy and immediately applied for a job as an undergraduate nurse in the city hospital. In our state there are no "undergraduate nurses" as such, except the students in the hospitals, so I had to become a licensed practical nurse. Having completed two and a half years in a regular nursing school, I found it easy to pass the practical nurses' State Board examination and easy to get a job. In fact I got the job before the license on the basis of the training.

I asked to work with polio, because I had been much interested in that disease since my own son had suffered from it. I wanted to keep abreast of all the latest developments in treatment to help him. He was not yet completely well, but walked with a limp because one foot had become slightly deformed. I asked to work the afternoon shift too, to give me more time with Butch, because I wanted to be a real mother to him. I wanted to take care of him myself. And I asked for the day off on which the group met, in order that I could attend all of the meetings. My supervisor was very kind and graciously acceded to all my requests.

Inwardly I rather hated being a practical nurse, and I could not bring myself to wear the green and white cap. I felt that if I could not wear the cap which was a symbol of my own school, I did not want to wear a cap at all. Of course, I could not wear my own cap (which was now the Fordham, or Cumberland, cap, since I had transferred to Cumberland school) because I had not graduated. So I wore none at all, yet strangely avoided the scolding from my supervisor which I probably deserved.

It was not that I had no respect for the profession of practical nurse, or that I held the cap in contempt, for I knew even then how valuable an aid the practical nurse is to the professional nurse and the doctor. It was just that I had worked so hard for something different. So might a doctor feel who had to work as a veterinarian. I remember the pride I had had when I received the right to wear my white cap, and what it had meant to me. I wasn't humble enough, I guess. But, wonderfully, the other nurses with whom I worked sensed how I felt, guessing, perhaps, by what they learned from me and from the nursing office of my story. They knew I had been in training and became ill and was still technically on "sick leave," unable to return to school, and in their understanding they were generous. Especially so was Georgia, a colored R.N. who became my good friend, but so were the other nurses, both colored and white. I know that they went out of their way to make me feel like one of them—that is, more like a student nurse than a practical nurse. And I was grateful.

And even more so was I grateful to the other practical nurses, several of whom were especially friendly. My pride did not antagonize them, as it might well have done, but they too understood and were kind. Most of them (colored) probably would have been registered nurses themselves if they had had the opportunity, but had become practical nurses because in our city there is no training school for colored professional nurses. But these nurses and most of the practical nurses I worked with, who had only taken the year's course offered by the city, were good nurses, and careful, and of invaluable help to the professional nurses and to the doctors with whom they worked. They certainly had nothing to be ashamed of either in their profession itself or the way they followed it. On the contrary, I could understand and rejoice with them in the proud way they wore their white uniforms, shoes and stockings and the little green and white caps. They had worked for those uniforms and caps with the same joy and hope with which I had worked for my own. So well could they rejoice in the accomplishment, and wear the symbols of their profession proudly. And as for those at least who worked in Isolation with me (for it is those I knew best) there was nothing second-best, selfish or mercenary in the way they gave themselves and their services for the patients. But there was a compassion and tenderness there, and generosity, which surely reflected the true spirit of nursing. In a few, in fact, it showed itself more here than in some of the professional nurses with whom we worked.

The doctors were all white, but the nursing staff, except the administrative staff, which was all white, was made up of both colored and white nurses, practical and registered. Nurse Atkins was one of the first colored R.N.s, or perhaps *the* first, to be employed, and had done so well that others had been employed. The white R.N.s and P.N.s were called "Miss So-and-so," the colored were called "Nurse So-and-So" (last name). Both colored and white "aides" were employed, though most colored "aides" were called "maids" and received a smaller salary. The "maids" did exactly the same thing as the "aides" (except the kitchen maid, whose duties were only in the kitchen; and the maids who cleaned up—these cared for the patients too, but in between the cleaning up).

The racial situation in the hospital was queer and mixed up, constantly changing, perhaps with the patients or the staff. When I first started, there was one dressing-room for the nurses, white and colored, and one for white aides; the colored aides and maids dressed in one of the utility rooms. Then one day I came on duty to find a separate dressing-room for white nurses and aides and one for colored nurses and aides. No explanation was given publicly, but a rumor had it that a white practical nurse complained about dressing in the same room and using the same facilities as the "niggers." I do know that afterwards there was one white practical nurse who had quite a bad time of it, both with all the colored and with some of the white nurses. Never had there been that type of segregation before, you see, not there. When Nurse Atkins had been employed, she had been accepted as a nurse among other nurses, and others who had followed had been accepted in the same way. Now maybe there were too many, and jealousy was rearing its ugly head. However that may be, there was something very shame-faced and apologetic in the attitudes of the white supervisors who worked in Isolation, for a while after that, especially when they were with Nurse Atkins. Many of us felt that they were being pushed into something in which they did not believe, or

34

were ashamed of believing. It was a cowardice with which we were all familiar; still we did not like them better for it, but less, and something happened to the respect which there had been before. Yet in a way, we too shared their shame, as we shared in their guilt by being unwilling to oppose the situation publicly.

As for the patients, there was segregation in the rooms, but not an obvious or painful segregation. The sickest children were all in private or semi-private rooms up and down the hall. This room might be white today and colored tomorrow. But the rooms on the ends of the hall were mostly for colored patients who were doing well and did not need special care. Still, it seemed to depend really on how many colored and white patients there were and how many rooms and vacancies. All the children (and the few adults) got the same nursing care and attention, so it was in this case really "equal but separate."

There was a television set given to the ward, and at first all patients who wanted to see it and had the doctor's permission, were taken out to see it together, regardless of race. Then a white parent complained, and for a while white patients were taken out one night and colored another. But almost all the nurses objected to this practice, it was too patently unjust. Finally it was changed again. The last time I heard anything of it, it was still unsegregated, but once prejudice begins making headway, as it did there, no one can say when or where it will stop. I don't know how it is now.

On the whole, working conditions for the nurses were pleasant. The salary, even of the practical nurses, was good for the South, the hours fair and the work, for those who like nursing, pleasant and not too difficult. The relationship between the white and colored workers in Isolation for the most part was friendly, congenial and helpful, even tolerant, save for the exceptions I have stated.

The white practical nurses, aides and students, observed an ethical regard for the authority of the professional nurse in charge, whether she was white or colored (often she was colored), and helped her and each other. The need of the patient did come, as it should, first. Seniority was honored where it really mattered most, in ward routine. The R.N.s worked a five-day week and the P.N.s a six-day week and both had time off for legal holidays. The food was not bad as such institutions go, and the colored nurses had a dining-room over in the main hospital which was very plain, but clean. Those from Isolation never went to it, but ate in the Isolation kitchen, by preference usually. It wasn't in any sense equal to that for the other nurses, but since we didn't go anyway, there wasn't much complaint on that score in Isolation.

For the maids and aides it was a different story. They did the hardest and dirtiest work and had one day off every two weeks. They were shamefully underpaid, making only about fifteen dollars a week. And although their dining-room and food were much worse than those of the nurses, colored and white, more was taken out of their checks for food. They had fewer holidays and sick days, and anybody was their "boss." There was little praise or regard for them, except from the patients, who at least could appreciate their worth for the comfort they gave, since they were really the ones who were often most with the patients who were not too sick in their most intimate and delicate needs, assisting, soothing, comforting, patiently encouraging. The children loved them.

Except for these three things, I liked the hospital. I liked the work and my fellow workers and supervisors.

I loved the children. Most were so brave in their helplessness, so puzzled by legs that wouldn't walk and hands that wouldn't reach out as they used to at the commands of little minds. Yet how well they accepted it, unquestioningly, without rebellion or bitterness—that was for the grown-ups. The faith one saw was amazing, and the generosity, in a world that often seems far from God. And the most heartening thing is that most win the fight back to health. Many people think of polio as always crippling or killing. It does do this, too many times; yet in most cases there is little, and often no crippling, after the disease. And the greater the faith, self-confidence, and strength of will of the patient, the more hope there is that there will be no after-effects. Most often it is those who give up who are permanently and badly crippled.

Sometimes we had fun too, when we were not too busy. Sometimes there were parties for the patients, as on Halloween or on birthdays. Other times, the nurses made candy or chocolate for themselves and the patients. Once I made candy and broke something and was so frightened I didn't know what to do. But a white student said she would take the blame, and she did, for coward that I was, I let her. She didn't even get a scolding though, as I certainly would have, so maybe it was for the best. I was very grateful to her. Most of us watched Arthur Godfrey on television with the patients too, when we had time, and the colored nurses and aides were very proud of the Negro talent on his show, and glad that the others could see.

I liked the job and the patients, and went because of that gladly, day after day, returning home tired but feeling good inside.

4

A MONTH OR SO BEFORE I WENT BACK TO WORK, BUTCH had to go to the hospital again for an operation on his leg, because that leg was still shorter than the other and was causing the foot to grow crooked.

I had expected it; still, it was very hard to take. He was such a little fellow, just turned four, and he felt so well, I knew he could not understand why he must go. But what made it hardest was the fact that no real hospital would take him. Color, ebony. There it was again. No matter how hard you tried to ignore it; no matter how you worked to forget it; something came to remind you of it, like a dash of cold water in the face or a punch below the belt. You wanted to forget, but everything reminded you: there are two worlds, two societies within one—a human society and one for the Negroes.

The city hospital takes Negro patients, but only in cases of acute illness or emergency. This was an elective operation, and the city hospital did not take that kind of patient, white or colored. There were three other hospitals, Baptist, Methodist, and the Catholic St. Joseph's, but they were for white only. The two tiny colored hospitals were understaffed by poorly trained people with totally inadequate facilities, unrecognized by the city properly as hospitals, not condemned by the board of health simply because there was nothing else, nowhere else for a Negro to go in such circumstances. Again and again the newspapers had campaigned for a better Negro hospital, but so far that was all that had been done.

The "best" one was dirty, smelly and infested with vermin—roaches, ants, bed-bugs and rats. It was crowded and, as I have said, understaffed, by those whose training (on the nursing staff) only made them eligible in the city for a practical nurse's license—yet here they were nurses in charge. This was where he would have to go if he had the operation.

In desperation I wrote to the Catholic hospital, telling them the situation and asking if some place might not be found there for a small boy. I certainly don't like being segregated; it hurts, even kills, something good inside you, but sometimes it's better than nothing. And I hoped that he might have even a Jim Crow room, out of the way somewhere, as is often arranged by such hospitals in the South—a hole in the corner, a side room in the basement. Any real hospital, I felt, was better than the one to which he must go.

I waited anxiously for the Sister in charge to reply, debating in a painful interior struggle whether I ought to refuse to let him have the operation and wait a while. Perhaps some day things would be different. Maybe he could have the operation in New York whenever we went back. It didn't seem urgent, a delay might not do any harm . . .

Yet, if it did? How could I bear the responsibility of

that? Suppose it meant refusing a possible cure for him? But in filth? Suppose he went and was worse off because of an infection contracted there in the hospital? Over and over, back and forth, around and around in my mind.

His white doctor sympathized with me, very hurriedly. I thought I sensed in him, too, shame. We are all to blame for what exists here. Did he know, I asked, what it was like? Yes, he knew what it was like, Dr. M. said, but there was nothing he could do. I could stay with Butch day and night and take care of him myself, but that was as much as the doctor could promise. Maybe, some day . . .

"Some day I'll be dead," I thought, despairing, wishing I could cry, to wash away that hard thing within me, "and Butch, too. We won't need it then."

At last a letter came from the Sister at the Catholic hospital. She was terribly sorry. She knew that the conditions I described existed and regretted them very much. Still, there was absolutely nothing the hospital could do. They could not admit a colored patient. She was sorry. "Perhaps some day . . . "

I hugged Butch to me quickly to hide my face, fiercely, in love and tenderness; then went upstairs, hurriedly, so Mother could not see my face until I could compose it. She knew whom the letter was from. She had been waiting too.

Upstairs I knelt beside my bed, hiding my face in its covers, trying not to feel what I was feeling well up and spill over within me.

"O, God, oh my dear God, I love You," I prayed silently. "I want to believe. I want to love as You love, to forgive as You have forgiven and still go on and on forgiving. But I cannot. I am empty. Help me. Help me not to lose my faith down here, but to go on hoping, loving, believing, for I am afraid . . . I am so afraid . . . "

And I was. For I knew if I lost that, there would be nothing left indeed. Yet suddenly I saw how easy it is to lose—no, to throw away—what one holds dearest. How close I was to it. Its nearness made me dizzy.

At last I felt strong enough to go and face my mother. "They won't take him." I said shortly. "I'll send him on to ——Hospital."

I don't remember what she said. I think she tried to cheer and comfort me. I know we agreed to stay, one or the other of us, with him, day and night, for as long as he would need us.

Shortly after my decision, we had a meeting of the study group, and the question of racial discrimination in Catholic institutions came up. I told of what had happened about Butch at the hospital. One of the members, a nurse at the Catholic hospital, said she knew about it already. They had discussed it widely, it seemed, and she said that the Sisters had no objection to caring for colored patients, but the doctors would not stand for a change in the present policy. The chaplain, too, she insisted, was working toward that end, but the doctors, being mostly non-Catholic, were beyond his reach. She was truly sorry, she said, but that's the way it was. Then we went on to the discussion of other things.

When the time came for Butch to go to the hospital, we had fun shopping for new pajamas and toys that he could play with in bed.

"You be a good boy and Mother will get you something real nice."

"Okay."

"The doctor is going to fix your foot so it will be strong like the other one; won't you like that?"

"Um-humn."

He was happy. He bragged to his friends about the cast he was going to wear on his leg and how strong he was going to be.

In the hospital I read and told him stories until it was time for him to go up to the operating room; then I went to find the nurse in charge. He was in a room with other children, and though the other children were not very sick, the room smelled terrible. The floor was dirty and unswept and everything drab and ugly. A sick child's room, I thought, should be cheerful.

At first the nurse offered the excuse that the smell could not be helped in children's rooms because they soiled themselves and their beds. But I had been a nurse long enough to know better than that. There was no odor there which clean linen and ordinary hygienic measures and nursing care could not have banished.

At last they agreed to put Butch in another room. I accepted that, but unhappily. I felt compassion for those children who had no mother there to plead for them, or whose mothers did not have the courage and were afraid —"If I complain, they may take it out on the baby." I felt a real pity and oneness with the big boy who was old enough to notice the odors and be made extremely uncomfortable by them. And while Butch was out (and after he returned) I tried to make him and some of the others a little more comfortable by bringing them fresh, cold water or caring for such other simple basic needs as I could under the circumstances.

When Butch came out from the effects of the ether, he was in pain, and kept crying. Since a nurse did not come, I went to look for one. It was about eleven at night, and the halls were dark, but there was a light at the nurse's desk. I went there and waited and waited, but no one came. I looked further and finally found the nurse on duty. She had been sleeping in one of the empty beds. She came with me to give him an injection to lessen the pain, and I persuaded her to let me administer it. He took it smiling and I kissed him for being such a "big boy." After that he slept quietly.

He was only in the hospital a few days. Every day Mother and I kept him clean and amused. We tried to make the other children around him a little more comfortable too.

When he came home, his leg was in a cast, but he felt fine. He played around as usual, happily dragging the leg behind him, as cheerfully as if he had never walked. I borrowed Rosemary's stroller and took him with me to the park and to fish, and people were kind. I was grateful for this, because I didn't want him to grow self-conscious and sensitive about his handicap but hoped he would learn to accept it. He seemed to be doing that quite matter-of-factly. We talked of it casually, trying to make him feel confident even as we made him realize what things he could do and what he must not attempt.

As he grew better, the cast came off and a long leg-brace replaced it. This, too, he accepted without complaint, and soon adjusted himself to it. In a little while he was climbing fences and trees in it and climbing the "monkey pole" in the park. As far as possible, I let him follow the other children in their activities, never saying "You can't try that" unless it was really necessary, though often my heart was almost choked with fear for him. He wanted to do everything he saw the other children doing.

Once, especially, I remember how afraid I was for

him, when he climbed in his brace high up in a tree and then couldn't come down again because of it. Finally I persuaded him to jump down into my arms, and he came down unhurt. However, I did not tell him he must not climb again. Instead I told him to be more careful and not to climb so high.

My attitude made a lot of difference, too. Again and again I saw, and still see, how much. For one thing, he has not been made to feel "different." On the contrary, I often marvel that he seems so unconscious of his handicap, and because of that very fact is overcoming it, the doctors say.

Sometimes he has pointed out other people who walk in an abnormal manner and asked, "Mother, what makes that man walk like that?" Apparently he is completely oblivious of the fact that to others his walk also seems odd. And for all of this I am thankful to God.

When I came home from church every morning, he would (and still does) run to me to be picked up and loved. How good it was to hear him say "Mother." How good, too, to see him run by himself, without crutches, so very well and healthy and strong, despite his illness, and so full of love and generosity and patience, perhaps because of it.

His problems and needs made me more and more aware of the problems and needs of other children. Gradually an idea was being born in my mind, a picture of a new kind of house of hospitality for children. It was all hazy and unformed, however, just a glimpse into shadows, but it was growing more and more clear.

5

DURING THE SHORT TIME BUTCH WAS IN THE HOSPITAL I grew to know Father Coyne much better. And I don't think that I really began to appreciate him until then. His church was the nearest one to the hospital, so I walked over there every morning when I was at the hospital at night, or stopped on my way when I came in the morning. Then after Mass I had breakfast with him in the rectory. He went to visit Butch in the hospital (how he hated the place!) and always asked about him when I visited him. But mostly we talked about the study group.

By then we had finished the Encyclical on the Mystical Body and were applying ourselves to a study club outline of the Mass. We had spoken rather generally of the liturgy and the liturgical movement. We had discussed, again very generally, the lay apostolate, and in this connection read Dom Chautard's *Soul of the Apostolate*. We had talked about conditions in our own city, of race and wages and marriage and family life, but still had confined ourselves on the whole to discussion and study. I still felt, and some others did too, that we should and could at least have more of a prayer life together, that we could, for instance, attend Mass together in a group more regularly, if not at different churches then at St. Anthony's. That would serve the double purpose of strengthening us individually and as a group, through the liturgical and sacramental life of the Church, and showing by our example the unity of the bond of love in the Church which transcends race. Most members either dissented or could not come. By this time some of the group were getting restless, tired of study and discussion. Father Coyne never said very much, and many members supposed, quite incorrectly, that he was far behind us in his grasp of what was happening. Now, as I began to know him better, I began to realize that we had underestimated him. He was a priest among priests.

He seemed to be growing a little discouraged with the group. I knew it was partly because he was unable to interest more colored people in it. There were a group of students at a colored college whom he had tried especially hard to interest, as he saw them growing more and more away from the Church and being drawn into an agnostic, if not atheistic, liberal interracial group which preached "action now."

How he loved his people, his parish! How it hurt him to see so many who were young and promising, losing their faith, throwing it away, selling it cheaply for an illusion. It made his Irish blood boil, but there was so little he could do. And what must have hurt most was the fact that so much could be traced directly back to that old devil race, the devil he couldn't drive out. (It must be one of those that can only be expelled by prayer and fasting. But people "have no time to pray," and diet instead of fasting.) He worked so hard, and could not reach his own, it was no wonder he became discouraged, I thought.

46

He often said that he could do more if he had *entrée* to many of the white circles which were open to the diocesan priests. But he was a "Nigger priest." To some, that was almost as bad as being a "Nigger."

He was disappointed too, I think, that he never could get his good friend and brother priest in the Mission to the Negroes, Father Joe, interested in the group. He could not, as we could not, understand the latter's disapproval. But he said, "Oh well, the work will go on, since it is motivated by the charity of Christ." He hoped the group would persevere and grow. He would do all he could to preserve it. Nevertheless, as we talked over our breakfast one morning, he shook his head. "Our Lord can work miracles, but that is not usually His way," he said with feeling. "These white people down here are—well—what you and Jim want to do is good, and ought to be done. But they won't listen to you. I believe Jim is sincere, and most of the others. Still, I can't help wondering about some. It will take a long time," he ended, "and lots of grace."

And I agreed with him. "Only," I said, "I don't care how long it takes. At least we are a step in the right direction. We are a beginning. After us maybe others will come, and because of us they may find it easier." I thought of my friend Father Meenan, something he had said once: "But grace is purchased by sanctity and sanctity by suffering," and added, "We might do some good, accomplish something real, but we may as well realize right from the beginning that suffering is not separate but an integral part of the way."

Father nodded. "Yes, it is."

The study group absorbed more and more of my attention as time went on and as I saw more and more need for the things we hoped to obtain through the group.

There was the problem of the faith: The Negro parish church I attended was empty on week days, and on Sunday the pastor wondered aloud where the absent parishioners were; always there were too many empty seats. The Rosary was said aloud during the Mass, and the congregation seemed unaware of the sacrifice they too should have been offering. Negroes went miles out of the way to the colored church when there were white churches within walking distance. White people did the same thing in reverse. It was as if they could not see the Church as One, Holy, and Catholic. In practice, at least, prejudice had taken from it its universal characteristics and made two Churches instead, one white and one colored.

There was the problem of the family: Salaries were so low among colored workmen that most wives and mothers I knew had to work to help out the family budget. It was not a case of wives wanting to work out of the home, but necessity. Children were left with relatives, with neighbors, and often alone or with older children.

A few blocks from my mother's house, where I lived, two children burned to death because there was no one to care for them while their mother worked. One was a little boy named Butch. I went to see the neighborhood where they had lived and went to the funeral because I wanted to write something about it for a feature column, "Looking Things Over," which I was writing twice a week for the *Memphis World*, a colored newspaper. As I looked at the tiny caskets I thought of my own Butch, surrounded by loving care and watchfulness while his mother worked, in an apartment that was warm and bright and cheerful. But these children had lived in an old garage with a big door which had to be fastened from outside with a padlock. There was only one window, high off the ground, too high to climb to, and a transom near the roof. It was dark and gloomy and unhealthy. There was an oil lamp for light because the place was considered unfit for electricity; it would be "too dangerous" to wire it. Yet a mother paid rent here because she could not find anywhere better to go. There was no room for them. In all her years of searching, will the Blessed Mother still find no room for her child? Two thousand years of Christianity—how long does it take?

There was no one to keep the children while she worked, so the mother locked them up alone so that they "would be safe," so that "no one could go in and harm them"—for it was a rough neighborhood. And while she was gone, one of them upset the kerosene lamp and turned the stuffy little room into an inferno. The neighbors could hear the children screaming inside, but they could not get them out because the place was not built for human habitation—or for escape. So the children died, murdered by the indifference of Catholics and non-Catholics alike who have tolerated these things, or who have lamented these things without doing anything about them. We sin by omission too, by the things we ought to have done and have not done.

We talked about this in the study group, and I hoped more than ever that these people at least would soon come to see that we must not only talk about the Christ-life in the world but live it, openly, so that all could see, and some follow. I hoped that these at least would finally see that suffering and sacrifice are part of that life in the world; even the sacrifice, perhaps, of the good opinion of our families and friends, and our sense of community with them, when they cannot understand these things. I hoped they would see that the life of the Christian in the world must combine study, prayer, *and action*.

I hoped too that finally from this group would come one or more who might be interested in opening with me a house of hospitality, to serve the needs of the poor as well as our own spiritual needs.

Peter Maurin had said: "We need houses of hospitality to give the rich the opportunity to serve the poor; we need houses of hospitality where Catholic thought can be put into Catholic action; we need houses of hospitality to bring the bishops to the people, and the people to the bishops; we need houses of hospitality to restore to institutions the technique of institutions."

More and more I could understand what he meant. More and more I felt myself drawn to his way of thinking and living. True, I was still working as a nurse and I sometimes found myself deep in nostalgic memories of student days, or misty dreams of a day when I should return to the profession I had chosen for myself. Nevertheless, more and more, even despite the fine arguments and excuses I offered myself, the conviction grew that even as I was choosing, so was I being chosen. That is, it became clear that nursing, much as I liked it and good as it is itself, was something *I* chose, and it seemed that God asked more than this of me, that *He* had chosen this other for me.

I still remained free to follow my own will or His, of course, in this matter. Yet it seemed to my that if my choice for myself was without fault, so was it without merit. Anyway, I knew I would have to follow His way, because love is like that.

6

THAT SUMMER I WAS VERY BUSY. I WAS WORKING WITH the study group, writing my book, *Color Ebony*, and working as an undergraduate nurse at Isolation Hospital, as well as trying to get re-acquainted with and be mother to my son. That makes a full day in anybody's language.

Sometimes my mother worried and fussed about it. "You'll be right back in the hospital," she warned me. "I wonder what Dr. Okerschmidt" (who was still giving me pneumo-thorax treatments) "would say to all this activity?" But mostly she encouraged me and tried to help me as much as possible. She knew that what I really wanted to do was to open a house of hospitality in Memphis. She even encouraged this. "But remember," she said one day, when we were in one of our discussions about a house of hospitality, "Butch is your first responsibility, that little boy over there. You've got to think of him first, whatever you decide to do." She stepped away from the stove to smile at him, and he grinned back.

I knew that. Father Meenan and Father Kirby had both explained it to me often enough.

"I don't think he can lose by it," I told her. "If Our Lord sees fit to provide through me for the needs of others, I'm sure He will not forget my own son. Then, too, the money I make through writing, I can divide between him and the house for anything special he may need. I am not afraid of that part. When I went back to nursing before, it was with the intention of assuring myself that I could support him. And what happened? I got sick for almost two years and couldn't support either one of us. It is as if Our Lord were trying to tell me that I can do nothing by myself but He can do everything in me. The best insurance is to trust God and depend on Him."

"That may be so," she admitted, "but you want to be sure."

I said I was sure. I even knew where I wanted the house to be—in St. Bridget's Parish. Part of the reason for this I could explain logically. It was a church in a mixed neighborhood. The pastor was friendly to colored people, though the church was a "white" church. Situated as it was, in another generation it would probably become a colored or an officially mixed parish—if the South developed as fast as that. In this event, the workers at the house would be in on its beginning, growing with it. If these were fervent Catholics who set up the liturgy as the standard of measure, the growth would be through the liturgy.

There were other reasons, as deep and convincing to me, but which I could not and cannot explain. Perhaps one could call it an intuitive conviction I had that the house belonged here. I don't know. Perhaps it had something to do with the spirit of prayer which lay over the church like a warm blanket. There are churches we enter where we know Our Lord is present in the Blessed Sacrament only by faith. There are others in which we are instantly made aware of His Presence by the spirit of prayer that warms and fills the place, as if many people—perhaps saints—have prayed there. It is not something one can put into words; if you have felt it, you know what I mean. St. Bridget's had that, whatever it is.

"That is one reason I go to St. Bridget's most of the time," I explained, "instead of our own parish church."

"I had wondered about that, when you stopped going to St. Augustine's," she said. "Is that the main reason, then?" (St. Augustine's was the colored parish church of our district.)

"I don't know if it is the main reason," I replied. "No, in fact I don't think it is. Mainly I go because it is nearer and more convenient. I can walk over there in ten minutes, but it takes me at least twenty or thirty minutes to get to St. Augustine's on the bus from the time I leave the house. Anyway, it really is our parish church, no matter what is said to the contrary. It is the parish in which we live. We are an organic part of it, even if it denies us. It is like my hand denying my foot.

"I go there to show that I don't admit the existence of two Catholic Churches established by God, one White and one Colored: but I believe in *one* Holy, Catholic and Apostolic Church. If I lived as close to St. Augustine's, or even nearly so, as I do to St. Bridget's, I would go there, because I would be in that parish, and it wouldn't matter that it was a colored parish, except in principle. But there are four closer churches than that, and we come nearer being in any of the other three than in that one."

Mother laughed. "I agree with you there," she said,

"you are right. But you know there are a lot of people who would say you are very wrong. Even Negro Catholics, like Richard."

"Oh, I know it. He and I were arguing just that point the other day." I told her about it, the memory of it still vivid in my mind:

"You should support your own parish church," he had said.

"I do support my *real* parish church," I had returned. "I live in this parish and I am a Catholic. At least in the Church, let us not divide Christ; that is to crucify Him all over again."

"I heard your argument," Mother told me. "I don't know what to say. Surely there is only one Catholic Church. Yet we are here in the South. We are Negroes; and there are those customs which have been handed down so many generations."

"But they are *wrong* customs, and maybe this is the generation which should stop their passage. Look at it this way. If the Negro keeps taking a back seat even when he's not asked to, and separating himself slavishly from others wherever he is, how are things ever going to change for us? How are white people going to know that I am like them in what I think and feel and want if they never see me but as a servant? How can I talk to others about the Fatherhood of God and the brotherhood of man if I act as if I don't believe in it myself? How convincing can I be to others when I can't convince myself?

"I go to Mass every day. That is a dollar forty cents a week car fare if I go to the colored church. Wouldn't that money be put to better use if I walked to St. Bridget's and gave it there? Then what about those who are poorer than we are; who can't spend that much a week for carfare? Now they don't go to church at all except on Sunday. Some wouldn't go during the week anyway, of course. But some others would if they had the example of someone else to show them the Church is One and the Mass is for all of us; our Sacrifice.

"It might take a long time. But you can see that is possible in the colored people of other denominations. Many Baptists and Methodists go several times a week to their church as well as Sunday. They are proud of their membership in the choir and in other church organizations. They read their Bibles and can explain to anyone what they believe, so much so that the Negro is supposed, by others, to be deeply religious by nature.

"Then they become Catholics, almost as if for a reward for their diligent search for truth. Then, suddenly they change. They scarcely come to church even on Sunday. They apologize for their inability to explain the simplest truths of their Faith to their friends. They don't belong to any organization in the church and they wouldn't think of trying to join the choir.

"Why? What happened to them? They have more now than they ever had before, in having the fullness of the Truth, whereas before they only had a part of it. They have the Mass and Our Lord Himself to nourish them in Communion. What happened?

"Part of it, of course, could be the Latin, I guess. Yet a lot of these are educated people and that certainly need not have been an insurmountable difficulty. A lot of the older people probably had to take Latin in school anyway. I know I did, and I certainly wasn't a Catholic. I think a lot of it is due to the fact that the stress here is laid on the wrong things. They wanted Christ; they looked for Him and found Him in His Church. But then, almost at once, they lost Him in a myriad of ghosts, superficial pretexts, and delusions so misty they can't understand the simplest truths of the Gospel. We stress the obligation of Sunday Mass attendance without really trying to get across what the Mass is. In fact, at St. Augustine's, it seems to me, we try our best to cover it up, to hide it so no one can guess it is the Sacrifice of Christ on the Cross repeated over and over again. A high school boy or a man waits until the priest begins, and at once starts the Rosary aloud and the congregation answers him, the words, not understanding what the prayer of the Rosary is either, because it is a way of praying strange to most of them—naturally, because of their Protestant background. How could it help but be? But they want terribly to fit in, to be a part of it all, to do the right thing, so they answer the words and maybe wonder what the priest is doing up there, if they can see him. They surely can't hear him, because of the Rosary.

"Or maybe, if no one is there to lead the Rosary, which is seldom enough, the choir will come in and sing songs that have nothing to do with the Mass or the feast. They don't explain anything or communicate anything; they are just songs. And again, the Sacrifice is hidden, pushed into the background as if it is of secondary importance in our eyes.

"Yet the laws of the Church say we have the obligation to go and we stress the obligation to those who have never understood it, and have never learned what the Mass is.

"Or we hear again and again that we must support our pastor. Every week there seems to be another need. Yet how often do we hear what the priesthood is, and what it means to us? We hear the names of saints and have saints offered for our veneration, but how little we hear about the lives of the saints! They aren't made to seem like men and women to us, and they are total strangers to folks six months removed from a Protestant upbringing in which they neither knew nor cared about those things. We hear of the deeds of the saints maybe, but how little of their love, which is the only thing, really, which made their deeds worth remarking. And we speak of the Church as if it were this building, or this group of people, and not the Mystical Body of Christ.

"And not only that. After speaking of its unity, we openly divide the Body—as if Christ could be made two—so there is not for us one Church, but two, one 'Catholic' and one 'Colored Catholic,' as the Sunday papers put it. Seeing this inconsistency, is it any wonder that the good Methodist should become a bad or fallen-away Catholic so often?"

"I guess not," Mother replied. "I've often wished Father would stress those other things more. There are so many little things I don't understand about the Mass, and about the Bible particularly. Father K. used to talk to me about this race business too. And I know he felt bad about it. Still, he said we should be patient as Our Lord was patient."

"That's true," I assented soberly. "For certain, we can't change the situation by getting mad or becoming bitter. We can only change it by love. But it must be a love that is all-embracing. It can't be frightened or proud. It has to dare and yet stay humble and know how to wait patiently; and it has to be centered in God. He must be first. That's the only thing that scares me when I think of opening a house. I'm not sure I have it."

"Then prayer will get it for you," Mother pointed out.

I leaned back and shut my eyes, for all at once I felt very tired.

"I know," I said, "but I pray so badly."

She did not believe me and I could not explain to her the violence of the temptations that sometimes assailed my faith, even during the Mass, at times, until I wondered, "What am I doing here? What kind of idiot can believe anything is happening here?"

Most of the times they were ghost-like phantasms of such indefinite shape I could not catch hold of them even in a word. Passing thoughts to disturb my peace of mind only, and my prayer. I don't think there was ever any real danger in them.

"Have you ever thought what you would do if you can't open a house here?" Mother asked thoughtfully then.

"Oh, sure, lots of times. Every time I go to Holly Springs to see Daddy, in fact. It seems to me then that the house might well be there. And even if I do start here, I know I want a farm down there eventually, near Daddy if possible, so he can help me, if he is not too much opposed to the house. There is a little piece of land down there, not far from him, that would be just the thing for a retreat house. Or there is another place, nearer the church down there. It is beautiful, with grass and trees and honeysuckle, and ground just begging to be planted. It's quiet, and in the spring you can smell the honeysuckle and hear the birds singing. I can just see our retreat house there."

I looked at her, smiling questioningly, waiting for her to answer and wondering if she were going to laugh at me. Instead she shook her head, a bit incredulous at my audacity. "Little girl, I sure hope you aren't disappointed in all your figuring. Things don't always work out just like we plan them, you know. You might be disappointed."

"Oh, I can't be. Don't you see? If this is really the work

God wants me to do, then He just has to make it possible somehow for me to do it, not for myself, but for His own Glory.

"As far as I am concerned, sometimes I dream of a different kind of life, with just me and Butch—or maybe, in some way, even a more normal family, with lots of children, such as I might have had if his father had been different or if I had been. And that is still possible too, you know. I'm still young. A lot of things could happen . . ."

I looked at her face and hastened to add, "Oh, don't misunderstand me. I want the house all right, and all that goes with it—the poverty, the suffering, the uncertainty, the misunderstanding that I know has to come because the rest of the family don't understand like you, and can't. But I only want the house and the work that goes with it because I am convinced God wants it for me.

"Sometimes" (and here I laughed a little, amused at my own inconsistency) "I almost wish I did not feel that so definitely, and wish I could convince myself that I am wrong in wanting this. Then I imagine it would be so wonderful to get up in the morning, go to church, spend a peaceful half hour or so in prayer, then come home and clean up and dress Butch." I spoke dreamily. "Then we could read or fish all day till time for me to go to work. I'd go and try to be the best nurse possible, and feel good if I could bring joy and comfort and health to my patients, or sad if I had to lose one, and could not make him better. I'd work so many hours, then I'd be through; I wouldn't have to worry about the job till the next day. On my day off we could spend the day together, and maybe study a little or discuss a little the problems of race and poverty and all that. I might even belong to organizations which would fight the injustices that make me so sick and mad now. But I'd have definite hours to work, and hours to pray, and hours to do what I wanted to do. And the same with my salary—so much money for this, so much for that, but this much just for me, for what ever I wanted, silly or not—and in my dreams, it sounds so wonderful, so normal.

"Then in the middle of it, the priest is at the altar and it's the time for the last Gospel. Sometimes all of it strikes me, sometimes just a part. But every time, one part comes to my mind stronger than anything I can describe. 'And the Word was made Flesh, and dwelt among us, and we saw His glory as of the only-begotten of the Father.' Then I know all those other things, good as they are and wonderful as they sound, could not be enough for me.

"Think of it, Mother, *The Word was made Flesh!* God so loved the world that He gave His only-begotten Son! What can compare with that? No wonder Our Lady could not say 'No' to the Angel. When I think of it, how can I help but say with her, 'Behold the handmaid of the Lord, be it done unto me according to your word?'"

"I understand," she answered, with a tender sigh of affection. "You could not, for sure. Don't worry. You'll have your house."

7

SEVERAL TIMES THAT SUMMER I WENT DOWN TO HOLLY Springs, Mississippi, to visit at the home of my father and my stepmother. I liked to go down to the peacefulness of that house to rest and think. Butch liked to go down and play cowboy and Indians in the hills, and to fish and swim in the pond. I always took one of his cousins or friends down with us, so he would have a playmate, usually Nathaniel or one of Rosemary's children. They liked it as much as he did.

My father had built a pretty little house not far from the corporation limits of the town, just far enough off the highway to miss the noise of its traffic. There was enough land for several nice gardens, and fresh vegetables and fruits were plentiful. Daddy canned the surplus, either alone or with the help of my stepmother, so there were shelves of delicious vegetables and fruits in jars. One room was always kept ready for our visits (my brother and sister, Butch and myself), which were usually spur-of-the-moment and unannounced. Besides this, we could read the books in Daddy's work-room and use his typewriter or duplication machine.

Or, if we did not want to stay in the house, there was a lovely spot outside under the trees by the pond, green and shady. There was a little hill for a back-rest, and in the spring you could smell the trees in blossom. The pond was shallow and dull with clay, but there were lilies growing there and tall grass like cat-o'-nine-tails. When it was quiet you could hear the fish jumping and the funny song of the frogs, "chug-go-rum." That was my favorite spot. One could pray there or "just think."

It was very quiet; only the small sounds of nature to break the silence of one's thoughts or meditations. Sometimes a red bird would flash by in a game of tag with its mate. Again a bluejay would come screaming a warning, as the puppy came running in pursuit of a rabbit and stopped to give me a friendly wag of his tail. The cow on the hillside would call mournfully every once in a while to her calf tied lower down in the pasture, and the baby would return her call with a plaintive "Maa-maa." Or one of the white hens would be bragging about an egg she had just laid, and a rooster boasting about his beauty and strength. Now and then Butch would run up to show me some interesting thing he had found, a pretty colored stone, a bright butterfly, a queer-shaped root or flower.

In the evening, Daddy and I would go into the living-room for an hour or so of music of our own making. Sometimes he would play the piano and I would sing, or Butch and I would sing; other times I would play the piano and Daddy would play the violin or trombone, much to Butch's delight. He would listen and watch, fascinated.

Occasionally Butch and I would go into town to see friends—such as Celestine Doxey—who had been children with me and who were now married with children of their own. Celestine's oldest child was Butch's age, so they always had a fine time playing together. While they played, Celestine and I talked, mostly about the children or about the little town where we had grown up. It had changed a lot in the years. Now there were several really nice colored restaurants, then there had been none. There were colored barber shops and beauty shops and a new school (Catholic) for colored children. The public school was improving, too, and improved. Belatedly the state was trying to raise Negro educational standards to the level of the white, before the bell tolled for the end of segregation. At last they were really trying hard to make the schools "equal but separate."

"It will take many million dollars," Celestine remarked.

"But for all that, when it comes, it will be too late. Equal but separate, even if it became a reality, is no longer enough. The time for that is past."

"And few will mourn its passing long. Helen, the world is going to be a lot different for our children than it was for us—you know that?"

"And I'm thankful. Remember when a colored person couldn't buy a first-class train ticket, but had to have a white man buy it for him, and then couldn't be sure he would really get to ride first-class? And remember how we used to have to stand outside in the cold and the rain to wait for a bus because there was no colored bus station?"

"That's not a whole lot better now, you know; we still have to stand outdoors at a little window at the white bus station to buy tickets."

"Won't they sell you a ticket in the colored bus station?"

"No, that's just a cafe and waiting room, while its

63

open. It's not open all night, so you still have to stand outside for the night buses, and they can't sell you a ticket."

"I didn't know that. I always buy a round-trip ticket in Memphis, so I haven't seen how they do it."

"But things are getting better. I remember when every store clerk called you 'girl' or 'aunt.' Now it's 'customer.' I remember when there was not a decent, clean place for a kid to go for a good time in the evening, now there are two or three."

"Yes, things are changing, faster perhaps than we realize. But still it seems slow. What is it they say? 'The last lap is the toughest.' I guess that must be true."

Most of our time in Holly Springs, though, was spent at home with Daddy. I liked to talk to him and listen to him. His advice was always sound. Following different lines of reasoning, we arrived at the same conclusions. One day, for instance, we got started on the labor problem:

"Here in the South," Daddy said, "the white and the colored must learn to get along together, or we will all perish. Mississippi is the poorest and most backward state in the union because white people have been trying so hard to keep the Negro from being anything, or having anything, that they have lost what they were and had. You can't keep a man in a ditch unless you stay there with him."

"I know that is true," I nodded agreement. "The poor white is the most prejudiced of all, with the least reason for it. He doesn't seem to realize that when people have slaves, they don't need hired men. Negro peonage does not make him richer, but poorer, even, than the Negro he

64

despises. The lowly jobs reserved for the Negro are many, if the pay is bad, but the jobs they want to think of as 'white' are much fewer and the competition stiff, so he is left with neither. Why should an employer pay him a living wage when he can get Negro labor for a song? The white man is afraid of Negro competition if all kinds of jobs were open to the Negro, but now he's not even in the running. If each job brought a living wage, sure, competition would be greater, but we'd all live better."

"Yes, you'd think they'd realize that, but prejudice is a blind god, and ignorance serves it well. But gradually things are changing. The other folks are beginning to realize that segregation is an awfully expensive luxury, and a terrible waste. I was interested to see some of those things this white editor down in—is it Greenwood, Mississippi?—has been writing—that man who wrote *Southern Legacy*. They are beginning to see that prejudice has hurt them only a degree less than it has hurt us, and in a different way. And now they see, too, that within the United Nations, the colored peoples of the world are watching to see what will happen to the Negro in America. When Americans talk about democracy and freedom to Communist countries, the Chinese, the Japanese, the Koreans, the Africans, all want to know 'What about the millions of Negroes in your own country who have not the freedom you promise us?' And there is no answer. In the end, there can be but one answer they will hear, the one which recognizes the worth of people for themselves and not their skin colors."

"I'm glad of that. The thing that worries me about the South is what it can do to Butch. I don't want him to grow up in hate and bitterness and envy, ashamed of his own race and hating those of other races."

"It is hard. But I think I did a pretty good job on you kids."

"I'm glad you think so, sometimes I wonder. I think, 'if only I could forget prejudice,' and I try. I go along, minding my own business, not hating anyone, thinking of other things. Then I glance up casually at a restaurant I'm passing and it says 'For White Only.' Or I see a movie I'd like to see, but that, too is 'White Only.' I say 'To heck with it.' I go on down the street to a store and stop to get a drink of water at a fountain. And there are two of them. One says 'For White' and the other says 'For Colored.' I change my mind. I'm not thirsty anymore. I think I'll take a bus and go home. When I get on the bus, a sign says 'Colored passengers to the rear. Please occupy rear seats first.' I take a seat on the bus and gaze out the window, feeling mean and trying not to. I see a whole block of houses with signs in the yard 'Not for Sale to Negro.' The signs don't even say that the houses *are* for sale to anybody else either. Just that they are not for sale to people like us. And I need all the faith I've got and wonder how you have stood it all these years."

"I had to learn a long time ago, when I was a little younger than you are now, that you can't do any good by getting mad. You only make things worse for yourself. I learned that the hard way, but I learned it well. You can't do anything with others until you are master of yourself. Whatever you do has to start with yourself. And we can't right things by acting wrongly. My grandmother used to say, 'Right never wronged nobody.' In the end, the right always wins out."

"I wish I could convince all the members of our study group of just that last part. Some seem convinced that you can do wrong for a right motive."

Daddy shook his head, negatively. "No, it may take more elbow grease to do things the right way, but that is the only way they ought to be done."

"That is another thing I wish I could get them to see, that it takes a little elbow grease too. Some seem afraid of work and suffering. We do have to study and pray, but if we do it as we ought, it seems to me that it can't help but lead to work. Some want to work, to act before they have the vision, before they know where they are going or why. That is bad. But it seems to me almost, if not *as* bad, for others to think they can have the vision and do nothing about it. The Wise Men saw the star, but they had to follow it to Bethlehem."

"It is slow work, getting other people to see these things. You have to be patient."

"Are you telling me!" was all I could say. I was silent awhile, thinking. Then I spoke again. "Yet you know, Daddy, sometimes you find those with the vision and the desire to do something about it but without the compassion and understanding it takes to reach other people."

I was thinking about the study group then, about some of the discussions we had had. One in particular I remembered frequently, because it had made such a vivid impression on me. We had been discussing marriage and the family and the question of "bad" marriages, or attempted marriages of divorced Catholics in other churches or by justices of the peace. How should we treat people we knew who had entered such states?

"The Church binds us in conscience to discontinue all friendly relationships with them, no matter who they are or how close they may have been to us before," one of the students said.

"That's right," another had agreed. "There are several

cases like that in our parish. These folks have a little money and a lot of influence around town, and that is what seems to impress the Catholic business men, because these lapsed Catholics are generous whenever there's a drive for money for school or coal, or what-have-you. People cater to them for that. Supposedly 'good' Catholics do business with them, invite them to their homes for dinners and parties and go to theirs in return. It doesn't seem to impress them that those people can no longer go to the Sacraments and that really they are dead to the life of the Church, even if they do come and sit through twelve o'clock Mass now and then."

"Yes," Joan added. "If we are going to be the leaven in our society, we have to show by our example what we believe about the Church and the Christian Family. It will be difficult, but we cannot act as if we were no different and believed no different from a pagan society."

Only a few of us had objected. "What you are getting at," I argued, "is all right, except that the question is much more complex than you make it. How can you in charity and without scandal drop all friendly relationships with the person next door, for instance? Even though he is spiritually dead if he enters such a marriage, I think we have to extend to him the common and accepted courtesies that go in our neighborhoods. Remember, we do not live in a Christian community, and here in the South where most of our neighbors are not Catholics and do not understand why, to us, a divorced person remarried is not really married at all, people will be gravely scandalized if they see us, purportedly good Christians, refusing to speak to the people next door or to extend to them little neighborly kindnesses.

"We can make our disapproval of a thing or an action

evident to everyone without snubbing people, or acting in a manner that our Protestant neighbors are sure to consider uncharitable. Besides this, I certainly don't think that kind of treatment will bring people back to the Church when they have left it to live in a state of mortal sin. Our Lord said, 'Judge not, lest you be judged.' It is not up to us to mete out the punishment for other people's sins. That is God's province. I think we have to make people feel that we love them still, even though we know them to be wrong, and that we understand, even while we don't excuse. That certainly makes it easier if they ever want to change, and much more likely that they will."

"It is not what you and I think," Joan contended, "but what the Church says. And it is the Church that says we must drop our friendship for people like that. They have cut themselves off from community; they should not be allowed to believe themselves still a part of the Christian community."

"I don't believe it," I insisted. "Where does the Church say that? Who is your authority?"

We asked Father Coyne what he thought. He said, "We have to use prudence in these matters. There is no set rule. Sometimes I think the way Joan and the others are advocating might be a good way; but then, as Helen says, we do not live in a Christian community; that makes a difference."

Finally the argument had been settled by a quote from the Council of Constance which upheld what Father had said. The Church does not command our action in these cases where an ordinary excommunication prevails, but counsels our discretion. We have to decide in individual cases and circumstances. But the argument showed us that we were still in basic disagreement on important issues and forewarned us of some of the difficulties we could thus expect if and when we undertook action as well as study. I now explained this to my father, and he nodded understandingly. "They are all good, clean young people," I said. "I don't think they are really so harsh; they just don't know what sin is."

"I don't know much about your faith," Daddy answered, "but I can say this, they don't know much about people."

Sometimes we talked on like this for long periods; more often we were interrupted by the children coming in for something to eat. Then we turned our talk to other things, while I fixed us all something. Getting meals was easy there for me, because of all the things from the garden, and the preserves.

We never stayed there more than a few days because I had to go back to work. But whether we stayed a day or two or three, those talks with my father always helped me.

8

WHEN THE TIME CAME FOR FATHER COYNE TO GO AWAY on vacation, we wondered where we could hold our meetings. That was quickly settled for us by the kindness of a friend we had made over the year, Sister Leo Marie at Sienna College. She helped us to get permission to use a school. We were very grateful to her for that.

By that time it was clear to all of us that the group would have to become more definite in shape and aim, and since most members were eager to begin work together on some apostolic project, it seemed that the time had come for action as well. We talked a lot about it.

Jim thought the group should develop into a leadership training program. He hoped that we could get one of the diocesan priests, or perhaps Sister Leo Marie, to help us embark on a rather extensive course of training and study for Catholic Action, following a definite program which he hoped we could outline with their help, then send a copy of the outline to the schools and parishes for recruits.

"Bishop Adrian has already said that the C.Y.O. (Catholic Youth Organization) is the official organ for Catholic Action in this diocese," someone told us. "He doesn't want any other group."

"And he is certainly not going to consent to an interracial group," another put in. "He intends to handle the whole problem of race slowly and with as little fuss as possible. He knows that the people down here aren't ready for it yet. He won't approve. I can tell you that."

Then during the course of a discussion one night, a woman whose name I have now forgotten suggested that, since the members of the group were interested in study as a long-range program and as action for now, we develop some project on or around Beale Street. As a group we could study the problems, then in this place we could put the things we learned into practice.

The suggestion was accepted by almost all with enthusiasm. What was proposed was a place where both the corporal and spiritual works of mercy might be practiced by all the members.

"It could be something like a settlement house," someone ventured, "or this house of hospitality idea you are always talking about, Helen. Maybe we could have a sort of day nursery for working mothers, or a community center or something like that."

"Yes, it would be wonderful if we could get a group down there of white and colored working together. That would be real Catholic Action."

"But we'd have to have a pretty well-knit group, thinking all pretty much the same way about methods and all, to start something like that," I objected. "We can't go into something like that and get people depending on us, then let the whole thing fall through because of differences in the group, or the unwillingness of some to do their share. We certainly can't open something like this if we are going to be afraid of families or friends knowing about our racial convictions."

"Oh, we all know that we would have to work it out. It would be a lot of responsibility, but that is what the group needs."

There was lots more discussion, and I found myself full of objections, though I could not have said why. However, I was easily overruled. Everyone was interested in starting a project along the lines of the original suggestion.

The next day I talked it over with my mother, trying to analyze my own unfavorable reactions. Mother was ironing and I was polishing my shoes to go to work.

"But I thought that was what you wanted," Mother said, "a house of hospitality down here around Beale Street, so you could go on working here as you did in New York among the poorest.

"You say they talked of a nursery—surely there's nothing wrong in that. If there had been a free nursery here, those children might not have burned to death a while back. I know a lot of children, like those over on the hill, who could go to school instead of having to stay home and mind baby sisters and brothers, if there were a nursery. There is nothing more needed here. I think Dorothy Day would agree that is so. Why couldn't a nursery be part of a house of hospitality?"

"Oh, that part is all right," I hastened to explain, putting down the shoes for a moment, and thinking; then, trying to put my thought into words: "It's a little hard to explain without being misunderstood. But you don't understand, and they even less so. You see, when I think of a house of hospitality, I think of a place where laymen or laywomen or both have gone to give themselves more completely to God through voluntary poverty and the practice of the works of mercy. I see it as a total giving of oneself, trusting in Divine Providence, and a real, wholehearted submission to God's Will. But they all plan it like a sort of social workshop and at the same time expect from it the effects of a house of hospitality. They don't really know what a house of hospitality is, even while they want to open one."

"Give it time," Mother advised, folding the piece she was ironing, "it might work out all right."

"Maybe," I replied. I was as doubtful as I sounded. I put on my shoes and dressed for work. "Anyway, I guess I won't discourage it any more until I see how it is going to develop. I just can't see how some of the members of this group are going to fit into the work of a house of hospitality with the attitudes they have on things like poverty, work, and personal responsibility. There is too much groupism in the wrong way. I don't know, of course. They are all nice people and they mean to do good. Maybe it will work out. We'll just have to wait and see."

At the next meeting it was clear that the idea for a house where the works of mercy could be exercised had caught on. There were three or four new people, and even they seemed to have caught the spirit of it. They promised to come back because they really wanted to have a part in the project, since they were well aware of the need around that area (Beale Street) for the kind of place proposed.

When Father Coyne came back, we continued discussing this project, and that of the leadership training program. The project, it was decided, was to be independent of the leadership training program, but affiliated with it. The two were to work together.

Father Coyne kept making one point as we discussed the project of a house where the works of mercy might be practiced: "There's got to be someone dedicated, someone who will be responsible no matter what happens or what the others do. You just can't jump into something like this. There has to be a leader, a head, for it. Who is going to be it, do it?"

At first the group was so busy talking about the project itself that no one paid any attention to Father Coyne's point. It didn't seem important to them. Gradually, though, a few began to understand what he meant and see that he was right, and ask, too, "But who will do it? There *has* to be somebody dedicated." Strangely enough, I think it was the new members who began to see this first, perhaps because our group had become so used to talking in indefinite terms, or generalizing. The new people were there looking for something concrete and were not going to settle for discussion.

Meanwhile, we were having serious difficulties in finding a priest to serve as moderator of the leadership training program. Most of the younger members of the group wanted a diocesan director, and none were available, but everyone we approached sent us back to Father Coyne. He said that he was unable, that he did not have the time, to act as moderator for the kind of group Jim had in mind. And the time was drawing near for Jim to go away to school. There was no one in the group that had anything near his interest in the leadership training program, nor his ability to carry it through effectively. He and Joan worked together trying to find someone for that part of our program while the days left before his departure grew shorter and shorter.

Discussion of the house continued. We all wanted a house where the poorest and most despised could find understanding and help. As a beginning, after much discussion, it seemed to us that the thing most needed which we could provide would be something like a combined community center and nursery. We could give out clothing to those who needed it too, and gradually expand our activities as we became more familiar with the situation and the need.

One of us would live in the place and be responsible for it; the others would help as they were able in various ways. The person at the house would get no salary but would get maintenance, and would try to become as much a part of the neighborhood as possible—except, of course, for its vice.

The others would work as volunteers, or otherwise help to support the work of the house. It was about this time that I volunteered to be the one "dedicated," *if* the house were going to be run on the principles of the Catholic Worker houses. For some that settled the difficulty of "Who?" But not for all. Some wanted to form a corporation of the group, with the group acting as board of directors.

At that suggestion—whether out of lack of humility or because of a foreseeing prudence God alone knows—I balked. I declined to be the one to go and live in the house under those conditions. I would continue to work at my nursing and would help, financially and in any other way possible for me, to support anyone else they could find to live there under those conditions, but I would not be the one.

The group showed a lack of unity of purpose and method too glaring for me to trust myself and Butch so totally to its hands at that point, I felt. And I had to think of him, too. So I explained that I would not go.

There was the question of finances, too. The same people who wanted the group incorporated to form a board of directors for the house also believed that we should take pledges or subscriptions, or in some other such manner assure ourselves of at least the monthly, or estimated monthly, running expenses of the house.

"We should have some guarantee of at least the basic expenses," was the way one girl put it.

Once more I protested. "We are not opening a hotel or place of business, and I do not see that it is necessary or even good to try to pattern our house after the ways and means of the business world. Is it a work of ours or a work of God's? All right. Then if we think God wants it, we should trust God enough to believe He will care for it without looking for any 'guarantees.'"

"Yes, but we must be practical, too," someone patiently explained to me. "Things just aren't done that way."

"Then maybe we should start doing them that way as an example to others. That would be a work of mercy, too. Besides, there is a supernatural prudence and supernatural way of being practical too, as well as a human one. And the supernatural is superior and ought to have first place.

"And it seems to me if we go around trying to 'guarantee' this or that, as if the work depended on us—well, then God might just let it depend on us, to show us how little we can do. But if we leave it to Him, that is the best guarantee we can have of its success, if He really wants it. And it would be a way, also, of telling whether or not He does really want it, because if it continues to be, depending only on His Providence, then He must want it."

Father Coyne agreed, but he added that it took faith to plan like that, and "It wouldn't hurt if you were assured of some support," he went on. "Not in the sense of a guarantee, because some people make pledges and then don't keep them anyway, but to the extent that it would encourage interest in the project."

Week after week the discussions progressed at each meeting and the project began to take more and more definite shape. It even had a name now. One of the Marys, I think it was, suggested Blessed Martin for a patron, because he was colored and had worked for the poor, and our work would be chiefly among the colored poor. I would have preferred "Peter Maurin House," because it was Peter's idea I had borrowed. But the rest knew little or nothing about him, so I was easily overruled. I did not insist because I didn't think Peter would have. And I had already told him in spirit, with a smile, "Since you got me into this by the things you wrote, I'm depending on you to carry it through, no matter who the official patron is. It's your idea, not mine."

I didn't know anything about Blessed Martin, but since all the rest were enthusiastic, I was willing to have him as a patron. He was a saint; that should be enough. And it was.

About this time the question of the leadership training program came up again. What was to become of it, if the Blessed Martin House project continued?

They were to grow up together, the response came at once. They were really a part of each other. The study and discussion would become puerile and sterile without the prayerful action of the house; the activity of the house might become a misguided activism without the prayerful study that was to be the basis of group discussions. That seemed to get universal assent, and we let it go for the time.

Meanwhile, the Blessed Martin House project had developed to such an extent that we were trying to decide on a possible location for the house.

Once again I explained that I had come to Memphis originally with the intention of finally opening a house of hospitality. For this reason, I had been on the lookout for the past two years for a place which would suit that purpose. In that time, I had come to the conclusion that the best place to start would be around the Beale Street area, because that was the street of need, and within walking distance from St. Bridget's Church.

"Why St. Bridget's?" The question was natural and came at once.

"Well, for several reasons. One is that it is on the borderline between a colored and white section of the city, and hence is ideal for interracial activity. Since both colored and white actually live in the parish, a colored and white group like ours could work together in it more effectively than in a definitely all-white or all-colored parish."

They wanted me to explain this, so I did: "You see, Butch and I spend a lot of time fishing. We meet a lot of people that way and make a lot of friends. I met a lot of people down there while digging bait from time to time. We start out by talking about fish and bait and go on to other things, so over the months we have gotten to know each other pretty well.

"Then another thing. They see me taking Butch to church a lot of times, and they noticed it when he started to wear a brace, those with children of their own especially. They started asking about him, and they have watched his progress with me and seem almost as happy, as he becomes able to do more things, as I am.

"All these are little things, but they would help tremendously if we did open a house in that neighborhood. The ice has already been broken, so a big part of our job is already done."

Some nodded and agreed. I continued: "Besides this, although it is a 'white' parish and church, colored people do attend it rather often now. The priest there is friendly to colored people and friendly to the idea of the house itself. I have talked to him about the possibility of opening a house in his parish planned like the Catholic Worker houses of hospitality, and he says he has no objection. He is not afraid of interracial activity, nor, apparently, the prejudices of his white parishioners, the way many pastors of white churches in mixed neighborhoods are. He is a Southerner and a Memphian, and if he became really interested, that would be much in his favor and ours."

Most of the group agreed that these reasons were too strong to be ignored, and we decided to try to find something in that parish if it were at all possible. We hoped we would be able to find something close to the church; but that seemed very unlikely because it was a very crowded neighborhood.

After some searching, however, we did find two store buildings for rent and a house for sale. The project was all too new and the group too unsettled to consider buying at that time. We were not enough at one in either aim or method, as far as the house was concerned. So we decided to look at both places for rent. Some of the men promised to go down and look at the places, and so did Father Coyne.

The rent for both places was outrageous. One was ninety dollars a month. It was brick and in pretty good condition, but it was in a neighborhood truly commercialized, and only a few dozen families lived nearby. Besides, it was close to a dangerous street intersection, and a little farther from the church than we hoped to be.

"We should be close to where people live," Father Coyne said, and we agreed.

The other store was seventy-five dollars a month, a frame building and in deplorable condition—dirty, unpainted, with plaster falling down and only one window that would open. The house leaned to one side, as if it were very tired after many years of looking upon human misery and destitution. You could put your hand all the way through the holes in the walls in some places, to the outdoor side. There was a vacant lot overgrown with weeds on one side, and shoddy two-room "apartments" upstairs. These latter were reached by rickety, rotten steps. It was all very ugly and uninviting.

But it was close to Beale Street and within easy walking distance from the Catholic church where the priest had been so friendly to the idea of a house of hospitality. It was in the middle of a congested neighborhood of cheap rooming-houses and bottled, littered alleys, and two-story tenement dwellings where children hung over broken porch rails or played with beer and whiskey bottles they had found in the alleys.

In the surrounding neighborhood lived many of the new friends Butch and I had made while fishing, and I knew I could count on them to be of some help, if no more than that of telling others about the place and re-assuring them with regard to our good intentions, on the basis of their knowledge of me.

When I first saw the "For Rent" sign, I was sure that this was it. I told Father Coyne. He agreed that it was just exactly where we wanted a house, where one ought to be. "But," he said, "I certainly wish it were in a little better condition. Half the floor is rotten and that falling plaster is dangerous." He had noticed (he couldn't help noticing), when he came to see it, how filthy the place was, too. "Do you think you could ever get it clean?" he wondered.

"If we worked at it with plenty of soap and water and disinfectant, I don't see why not," I replied. "Then, we could make the landlord do a lot of the cleaning, too. I don't imagine too many people are anxious to rent it, and I'm sure anyone would make him clean up first, so he will have to do that much. We could make him fix the floors and probably do a lot of other repairs as well. And what he won't do, I think we could. It seems to me that the most important thing is that it is exactly where we want it to be. What is it doing down here for rent if it is not for us? The people around here live in it, and other places like it, because they have to. It shouldn't be too much to choose to live so, voluntarily, for the love of God. I think in the beginning we have to realize—the whole group—that sacrifice and inconvenience are an es-sential part of the work, and of the ideas behind it. We aren't going to be looking for comfort and convenience in a house of hospitality."

"That's true," Father Coyne agreed, and I went on: "Peter Maurin's idea was to feed the poor, clothe the

82

naked, shelter the homeless, *at a personal sacrifice*. That means we aren't going to expect things to be as we think they ought to be, the way they are at home. He said that pagans watching the charity and mutual aid between the early Christians used to say: See how they love each other; but now, he says, looking at our indifference and our organizations to take over our responsibility for the poor, they say: See how they pass the buck. What we want to do in the house is to restore the right way of looking at things, and show our love by the way we live and what we do."

He said, "That is a strong argument, and after all, you are the one who is going to live there." He shook his head a little, though, and wondered aloud whether we could ever make it even barely habitable. Then he smiled. "It's funny," he said, "how many people, even priests, are afraid to stick out their necks for the betterment of their people. It's the old story of 'prudence.' What sins are committed in its name! But it is the poor, ordinary man who is the backbone of the Church. Some may call us radicals; yet we are mild in comparison to the popes. And just to help one person to a better way of life and to knowledge that he is important in the eyes of God is worth all our efforts. The work will never be an easy one, but God will bless your confidence in Him. He must. So if you are willing to go ahead, I'm with you."

That was enough for me. I smiled back, feeling a great peace.

9

By now the project had become so definite an entity that it became necessary either to seek episcopal approval or to decide definitely to go on without it. There were those who still felt so certain that the Bishop would neither approve the project nor give his permission to open the house that they were unwilling to ask it, lest we lose what we had and have to discontinue even as a study group.

But others of us were equally certain that we could get no support from Memphis Catholics without his support, even though, strictly speaking, we did not need his permission to open the house as long as we concerned ourselves solely with the corporal works of mercy and left out discussion and teaching and those like things which belong properly to the Church, to her teaching authority. But that was just what I did not want to do. If all I wanted to do was to relieve suffering, I pointed out, I need not open a house of hospitality to do it. That was my vocation as a nurse. A house of hospitality was more than that. Peter Maurin had spoken of the Catholic

Worker movement as "the Green Revolution." He had not wanted to start a Christian renovation to patch up society's wounds, but a Christian revolution. He wanted to build a new society in the shell of the old with the philosophy of the new. He said, "We need houses of hospitality to give to the rich the opportunity to serve the poor . . . to bring the people to the bishops and the bishops to the people . . . to make the scholars into the workers and the workers into the scholars . . . to bring back to institutions the technique of institutions . . . to show what idealism looks like when it is practiced."

So what I saw in a house of hospitality was more than a certain way of giving, a certain way of serving: it was a certain way of living. That was not so of the others. Some saw it as a project worthy of their support and assistance in their spare time, as long as it did not offer a threat to their personal lives on the job and in the family. They knew that their families would not understand and would object to their becoming too seriously involved in any interracial, or even "radical," social projects among the poor. And they did not want to disrupt the peace and harmony of their homes for anything like this. However, they were willing to help in the other ways they could, the other ways which did not offer this threat.

We discussed the question of approaching the Bishop again. There were still a few who objected to this for one reason or another, chiefly because most were so sure he would not give his approval to the project. "He is much too conservative," so many kept telling us. "He certainly won't stand for anything like what you have in mind. It is no use going to him."

But if I were going to take Butch and live at the

proposed Blessed Martin House, quitting my job and burning my bridges behind me, so to speak, I knew I had to talk to the Bishop about it and get his approval. That seemed to me one of the best ways to tell if God really wanted the house here: that it should be opened, or not opened, in obedience to our own shepherd, the spiritual father of all who lived in this diocese.

Father Coyne agreed, and after they understood, so did most of the others who had wondered aloud about it. So we decided to sum up in writing what the house would do and why it would exist, our aim and purpose. It should be clear enough to show him what we really had in mind, yet general enough to allow for growth and change as our understanding and ability to handle the problems increased. It should attempt to express the motivating spirit of the work.

The following Sunday we were having a day of recollection at St. Anthony's, with Father Coyne giving the conferences. In the intervening days, I had written a summary of what seemed to me the principal aim and purpose of Blessed Martin House, in a form that I hoped was concise, yet understandable, with quotes from some of the Papal Encyclicals to show where we got our ideas. In the group meetings we had talked about nothing but the house for the last few months, so I had no doubt that it was a true summary of what the group had decided they wanted to support, each member according to his ability and desire. Just to be certain, however, I got in touch with all the members of the group who were still attending the meetings with any regularity and reminded them of the decision to approach the Bishop. I told them about the platform and asked them to be sure to come on Sunday for the day of recollection, because afterward we were going to discuss the platform.

Sunday was a beautiful day, clear and sunny. Father Coyne had a high Mass for us, and afterward there was a small breakfast. We had planned a big dinner in the afternoon after the last conference. I gave Father a copy of the platform before Mass, in order that he should have plenty of time to look it over during the day. In its final form it read as follows:

WE BELIEVE with Pope Leo XIII that "the Catholic Church, that imperishable handiwork of our all merciful God has for her immediate and natural purpose the saving of souls and securing our happiness in heaven. Yet in regard to things temporal, she is the source of benefits as manifold and great as if the chief end of her existence were to insure the prospering of our earthly life." (*Immortale Dei*)

WE BELIEVE with Pope Pius XII, whom we love with filial affection that the human race has the "unity of one common origin in God 'One God and Father of all, Who is above all and through all and in us all (Ephesians 4:6)'; in the unity of nature which in every man is equally composed of material body and spiritual immortal soul, in the unity of the immediate end and mission of the world; in the unity of dwelling place, the earth, of whose resources all men can by natural right avail themselves to sustain and develop life; in the unity of the supernatural end, God himself, to Whom all should tend; in the unity of means to obtain that end." (*Summi pontificatus*)

BECAUSE WE believe these things, we are opposed to all ideologies in our society, defined or not, which ultimately tend to the dehumanization of man or to his loss of dignity as a child of God or which put intolerable obstacles in the way of his obtaining those things which are his by natural or Divine right. We are opposed to social and racial injustice which would deprive a man of these things because of the color of his skin or his economic status.

WE PROPOSE AS AN IMMEDIATE PROGRAM:

The alleviation of the immediate needs of the poor and indoctrination by example through voluntary poverty and the practice of the works of mercy, corporal and spiritual.

Clarification of thought through articles, discussions and meetings.

Houses of Hospitality in every poor parish to practice mutual aid, hospitality and charity, houses which would also provide workshops where the unemployed could become employed and the unskilled become skilled.

Farming communes and Christian communities where the communal and private aspects of property could be restored in accordance with the teachings of Pope Leo XIII; "Private ownership, as we have seen, is the natural right of man and to exercise that right, especially as members of society is not only lawful, but absolutely necessary . . . Man should not consider his possessions as his own, but as common to all, so as to share them without hesitation when others are in need . . . Whoever has received from the Divine bounty a large share of temporal blessings, whether they be external and material, or gifts of the mind, has received them for the purpose of using them for the perfecting of his nature and at the same time, that he may employ them as a steward of God's Providence, for the benefit of others." (*Rerum novarum*)

Father Coyne must have read it at once, or just after Mass, because while we were in the kitchen cooking breakfast he came back to tell me that he liked it and thought that it summed up well the aim and purpose of the house as it had been discussed in the group meetings during the past months.

The conferences were good on the subjects of poverty, charity, and trust. At the end of the day, at dinner, we talked about the platform of the house. There were just a few there, but they all thought it good. Because so many were absent, however, I did not want to send the copy to the Bishop yet, but wanted all to see it. With this in mind, then, the next day I called up all those who were regular in their attendance at the meetings of the study group, except one or two who were out of town, and read it to them over the telephone to get their opinions. Since these offered no objections either, I mailed a letter and a copy of the platform to the bishop of our diocese.

After that there was nothing we could do but wait for his answer, and this we did, with much trepidation and apprehension, hoping that he would at least give us a hearing before he said "no."

Meanwhile, Wednesday night was the night for our regular meeting at Father Coyne's, so we planned to discuss the project further.

There was a larger group at the meeting than there had been in some time. In addition to the members who had been most regular in attendance there were several old members who had not been there in some time, four or five new white members, and even one new colored member, much to my surprise and pleasure. She was one of Father Coyne's parishioners and he had interested her in the group.

At once talk turned to the proposed house. With two exceptions, all present seemed most interested in that. Joan mentioned the leadership training program and asked what we were going to do about it, and one of the men said, "We can talk about that later, when we get all this business about the house straightened out. That is the most important thing right now."

This was seconded by several, and Joan didn't say anything more about it. The men who had been down to look at the stores told the group what they had seen. They liked the neigborhood and agreed it was the place the house was most needed, but to most it seemed a little too poor. "Can't we find anything better than that?" they wondered. "The rent is too high for any building in such bad repair."

"That is true," I spoke up. "But the rent in any building intended for commercial use is going to be the same thing. That nice place is ninety dollars and the other seventy-five."

"Well, couldn't we get a real house instead?" someone else wanted to know. "That would be ideal," I admitted. "But in Memphis, in colored slums like that around Beale Street, there are no houses for rent. The houses are already full, with at least two or three families in them and others waiting to come in when those move. It is almost impossible to rent a whole house in a neighborhood like that unless there is something very wrong with it. And we would need a whole house."

"Oh, yes, I see that," came the reply.

"That house for seventy-five dollars might do if you could get the landlord to make some repairs, but can you?"

"I don't know. I know he would have to make some, but just how many I could not say. I just don't know."

"You ought to find out," another person said.

"Some of the men here should be able to help with some of that repairing," one new man said, "and maybe get some other groups in our parishes to help us. Surely for a work as important as this, we ought to be able to find men who would volunteer time or materials to help." He looked around but no one said anything to that, and he added, "My wife and I will do all we can to help."

"I don't have time to come down and be much help in that way," another man put in, "but my wife and I are behind it a hundred percent and we will help in the ways we can."

The discussion continued in this vein and ended by my promising to find out from the owners more about the repairs, and other members of the group promising to look around for other available places.

At the next meeting, the following week, I told the group what the owner had said about the repairs. He was willing to do the most needed things, like repairing the floor and painting the frontroom, fixing the cracks in the walls and adding a window and a new toilet, but he would not paint the outside nor do a lot of other things that needed to be done, such as moving a big ugly fountain or replacing the ancient cook-stove he had in there. He'd put new paper on the wall of the little room, he said, but he wouldn't paint the rest of it.

"It's too bad we can't find something better," more than one member said.

"I sure wish we could," I returned, "but we have to start somewhere, and it may be that once we have actually started, and people can see what we are trying to do as well as hear us talk about what we want to do, we can get more help. If other people see us trying to do something worthwhile with a little of nothing, they may be inspired to help us get something better. But so many people talk about what they want to do, and about what ought to be done, that it is hard to get people interested in projects like this until they can actually see something concrete. It seems to me that if we start where we can get a place, we can always keep looking for something better, and then we'd probably have more people to help us look."

"She has something there," one of the new members remarked, "and it might work out like that. After all, she's the one who has got to live there, and if she's willing to take a chance on it, I think we ought to back her up."

Joan interrupted the trend of the discussion at this point. "What about the leadership training program? Have we forgotten that altogether?"

"No, of course not," I said. "Isn't that a part of the same thing? Once we get the house, we will continue the study group as it always was. The program of study, prayer, and discussion will be just as important a part of the house as the works of mercy."

One of the new members did not understand that. "I don't know. We can take part in discussion groups and things like that in our own parishes. We don't need a Blessed Martin House for that."

"Yes, but the house is going to be the visible evidence of the things we study and talk about in the group. The members of this group will support the house, each in the measure he wants to and can. Some might give time and labor, or money, or all three; it is all left up to the person, how much he will give."

"Well, don't you think we ought to have *some* sort of a corporation or something?" Joan said, "like a regular business?"

"No, I don't," I said (not for the first time). "We are not opening a business but a house of hospitality. The house should be directed by those who share in the work of it, in the proportion in which they share it. The group as a whole ought to act as advisor to the house, and Father Coyne, of course, as spiritual director. That way, no one is forced to take more responsibility than he wills, and each can take as much as he wills."

"But back to the study program," one of the Marys said. "Some of us are mainly interested in that and can't get too involved in this house business as far as forming some sort of corporation, and owning property and things like that are concerned. So for us, how will the program be developed?"

"We will continue our regular meetings, but at the house, as part of it."

"Don't you think it might be dangerous or cause trouble if white women come down there to a meeting?"

"No, I don't think so, no more than here. A white woman in a colored neighborhood is much safer than a colored one, especially down here. A colored man is going to be awfully slow to touch you or bother you in any way, because he knows the penalty for that. No one but myself and my family and friends is going to care much about anyone bothering me, though," I said. "So if there is any danger there, it would be toward me rather than any of you. In fact, that is one reason why I hope we can have the meetings there. It will be a sort of security measure for me and Butch. People would be slower to bother us then in the neighborhood, even though they know we are alone and unprotected."

"That is very true," Father Coyne affirmed. "I think it would be safe enough to have the meetings there unless some neighbor objected to the interracial aspect of it. Then our trouble would be with the police rather than any other; but I really don't think that will happen."

"Who's going to direct the meetings, then, if we have them down there?" Joan wanted to know. "Do you intend to lead the study program too?"

"If there is anyone else who wants the responsibility," I said, "they can have it, but if not I am willing to try."

"I see," Joan said.

"Back to the house." (Another new member spoke now.) "I still think we ought to have some definite system for raising money every month. I think you ought to be guaranteed at least the basic expenses every month."

"Well," I said, "there's nothing to keep members of the group from planning things to help raise money for the house, and I think we all ought to give what we can to help it if we want it, but I don't think we can or should look at this in the sense of guarantees. If God wants the house to be in His Divine Providence He will see that we get the support we need. A more important thing for us to worry about is how we can see that the work and the spirit of the house are what they ought to be. That is our part."

"Well, what about Pacifism and all those other things that the *Catholic Worker* promotes, which are so much like Communism? As head of the house, would you promote those things?"

"I don't know what you mean exactly, because the *Catholic Worker* is not Communist. If you mean would I fight for just wages, and racial justice, and things like that which the *Catholic Worker* fights for, yes, I would. I believe in those things, and in this I follow the spirit of the Church and the Pope, as Dorothy Day does, because the Pope also strives for these things. As far as Pacifism is concerned, in a house like ours is going to be, probably dealing mostly with children, I doubt if the occasion would arise very much for it to come up. If it did, however, I would feel obliged to explain my position, just as I have in the group. No one else, of course, has to adopt the same position. Even in the house in New York, not all are Pacifists."

"It is getting late," one man said. "I think we'd better get together. As I said before, my wife and I will help all we can."

"Yes," someone else said, "and we will too. I think we can support the house to the extent that we believe in it and that it accomplishes good. All of us do not have to agree with every single thing Helen believes. We all know there is a need of the work. That seems to me most important."

And so the meeting ended on that note. We said Compline and the meeting broke up.

10

WHEN I REACHED HOME THAT NIGHT, AND ROSEMARY WITH me, the letter from the Bishop was there waiting for me on the kitchen table. It was only a short note, handwritten and friendly, ending simply, "Your idea sounds laudable and could be made practical." He invited me to come to talk to him about it the following Sunday at St. Peter's Orphanage.

I was so happy I did a little dance in the kitchen and hugged Rosemary. "Isn't that wonderful!" I exclaimed joyfully. "He doesn't sound at all like I thought he would! Why, he sounds nice! Oh, Rose, maybe he will say 'yes!'"

She laughed, too, and was as delighted as I. We talked about it for a long time, until it was so late she had to go home.

The next day I called Father Coyne and told him. He was as delighted, but not as surprised as I had thought he would be. He seemed to have expected it.

I then called Alice and several other members of the group and told them. I asked Alice and one or two others to go with me to the conference with the Bishop. The others excused themselves, but Alice accepted. "Now we won't have to worry about a way to tell him that the group is interracial," I said. "He can look at the two of us and see."

That had been one of our problems, how to tell the Bishop we were interracial without appearing to accent that side. We might emphasize again and again among ourselves that we were incidentally interracial, but the race situation being what it is in the South, it did not seem that we could ever be convincing to others. They saw only the racial side and became frightened and were unwilling to consider any other. We were afraid the Bishop would be like that too, and refuse his permission on those grounds. Yet we could not compromise, as Our Lord would not compromise but died for all, and lived for all, and loves us all as members of His Mystical Body. We were incidentally interracial in one sense, but necessarily so in another, to show our belief in the universal character of the Church.

Now that problem was solved, though. If Alice and I went together, the Bishop could see for himself what we were, then hear what we believed.

Sunday saw a very nervous and timid couple waiting on the steps of St. Peter's Orphanage. Alice was dressed in a dark dress, very simple and beautiful. She wore a dark hat and gloves. The tiny freckles on her high cheekbones were covered with a trace of powder, and she looked very cool and sophisticated. No one would have taken her for the mother of five healthy children. But that was because they could not see the kiss that Mary and Clare and the twins had left in the corner of her smile, or see where baby fingers had lain lightly in her lap.

I wore my nurse's uniform and a cape, because I had

to go on duty from the orphanage. The starched white and professional coolness of the uniform gave me a false illusion of self-composure. Actually, I was shaking inwardly.

I was a convert of only a few years, and the only time I had ever seen a bishop was at my Confirmation where I had been one of many. I think about a hundred. How would I greet him? What would I say? For two days I had practiced kneeling before him and kissing his ring (feeling very foolish as I did so), in order that it might not come so awkwardly to me.

At last a little Sister opened the door. "I am Helen Caldwell," I explained, " and this is Mrs. Hanrahan. We have an appointment with His Excellency, Bishop Adrian."

Sister smiled. "Won't you come in?" she invited. And as we followed her into a little sitting room, "Please sit down, and I will get him for you."

After she had gone, I turned to Alice. "Are you afraid?" I asked inanely. "Nervous, I mean?"

"Are you kidding?" she responded. "This is just as hard for me as for you."

"Do you think he is going to be opposed to us because we are interracial?" I wondered aloud, "or scandalized because of my ideas on poverty?"

"I don't know. You hear so many things. I just don't know. I hope he will understand. I've met him before, at Sienna, and he seemed terribly nice. I have heard from some that he is a very humble man. But I just don't know."

"We ought to say a prayer," I suggested.

"Yes, how about that one Father Coyne always says at the meetings?"

"Yes, that is to the Holy Ghost. Let's say it."

It was the feast of Christ the King. Under that title Our Lord was patron of my group in the C.U.S.A. I hoped that this was a sign in our favor. In the light of the Bishop's note, I dared hope it was. But I was afraid to be too confident.

"Oh my God, and Best Beloved, as You are King of all the earth and heaven, let him see that You are King of the poor, and of all races, and give us his blessings for this work—if it is truly Your will that it be started," I prayed over and over again silently; "that Your kingdom may be extended, and Your own name be glorified."

I knew that I could not please God by disobedience to His Church and that I must abide by whatever decision our Bishop made concerning the house. How afraid I was that he would misunderstand my fumbling explanations and never give it a chance. If I could not convince even the "radical" intellectuals of the study group, who prided themselves on their radicalism, how could I expect to convince this shepherd of souls noted for his prudence and conservatism? If I seemed imprudent and presumptuous to some of them, how would I appear to him? I was in an agony of nervous trepidation. Yet I kept praying, "Oh my God, if this is Your will for me, then make it possible for me to carry it out. I want to serve You in love, but only through obedience, because that is Your way. Help me, then, as You are my King and this the father You have given me, to convey what I know I can only say badly. Please, please."

And I said with Alice in a whisper, "Come, Holy Ghost, and fill the hearts of Thy faithful and enkindle in them the fire of Thy love. Send forth Thy spirit and they shall be created, and Thou shalt renew the face of the earth." We prayed softly together. "In the name of the Father and of the Son and of the Holy Ghost. Amen." We made the Sign of the Cross over ourselves.

We smiled at each other and took a little courage from the words while we waited. Then he came in.

I don't remember all the details of that meeting, but only impressions and phrases of what he said. He made the formalities easy. He was so very humble and gracious. I remember he had white hair, and his blue eyes were very kind and gentle. The priest shone through his smile and the way he talked. I was no longer afraid of him after a few moments and found myself talking to him easily about the group and the proposed house. I explained the platform and its inspiration from the Catholic Worker and told him frankly about the difficulties in agreeing on a place and a way of support. I tried to explain my convictions about poverty, and whenever I hesitated or stumbled, Alice came to my rescue. She explained how some people believed we should have some guarantees of support, and how it seemed to others of us that we should trust in the Providence of God. We hoped he would not think us presumptuous.

Wonderfully, he understood. To my astonishment, he understood better than anyone else ever had since I had come to Memphis, better even than Mother or Alice or Father Coyne had. He encouraged us warmly with a wonderful sincerity, and when I was lost for words to express my meaning, he himself expressed it with a simplicity which I had never been able to achieve in trying to convey my ideals to the other members of the group.

He reminded us of Our Lord's parable about the birds, which do not gather and store into barns, and the flowers, which trust God to clothe them, and reassured us of the *prudence* of trusting God to provide for His own works. He was not afraid of the interracial aspect of the program because this was a part of the universal aspect of it, the

Catholicity of it. We were interracial because we were Catholics and race did not matter to us. He was not afraid of the possible implications of our loyalty to either Friendship House or the Catholic Worker, as so many lay people had been who had been a part of the study group. Instead, he was able to discuss these things with us in a friendly manner. He did not oppose the study program, but he was much more interested in the development of the house and the example of Christian living which he considered it would give. He believed that would be much more effective and important than the things we could discuss or teach. He gave a tentative permission for us to invite priests from his or even other dioceses to speak to the group in the ftuure if we desired. He hoped we would emphasize the other part of the work more, however.

He talked to us about a group in Italy which had just such a humble beginning as our house and which had grown into a great work pleasing to God and serving thousands of people daily. He hoped our house would follow its example.

He didn't want us to be afraid but urged us to persevere in our trust in Divine Providence, and gave us several incidents from the lives of the saints to make his meaning more clear.

"In a sense, Our Lord has obliged Himself to provide for us, when we depend on Him and do His work," he said.

We were filled with a great peace of mind and joy at his words. I felt new courage, because the opposition from so many people who were so much better and wiser than I had begun to wear me down and make me wonder if after all I could not be deceiving myself.

We asked him then if he would appoint Father Coyne to be our moderator, since he had worked with us for so long. He promised to do it. Then we knelt down before him, thanking him, and asking him, "Now may we have Your Excellency's blessing, for ourselves and for Blessed Martin House?"

"Of course," he told us. And he raised his hand over us to give us the blessing of Christ, through His Church, on the work.

That night there was a dinner of some kind, and most of the priests of the city were present, together with Bishop Adrian. There he saw Father Coyne and told him of our talk and appointed him our moderator. So he kept his promise.

Father was jubilant with us, and surprised that things had gone so well for the house. In fact, I think his own faith in the possibilities of the house grew from that day. Before, he had been helpful, encouraging, and willing to give the house every chance and the benefit of all doubt, but still he had been a little skeptical too, a little unconvinced.

I could hardly wait to tell the whole group about our meeting and its results. I could imagine how surprised and pleased they were all going to be.

It was just at this point that the first of the letters came.

11

I WAS VERY HAPPY AS I OPENED THE LETTER BECAUSE I COULD tell by the address that it was from one of the white members of the group who had not been to any of the recent meetings but who I knew was nevertheless very much interested in the group's progress; a person for whose opinion I had a very high regard, and who was a very good friend of mine besides.

But my happiness was short lived. As I began to read, a sort of stunned incredulity took its place:

Dear Helen,

. . . You have acted in a selfish, individualist, arrogant, dishonorable and impetuous manner . . . I have learned from unimpeachable sources that you have . . . taken the Blessed Martin thing out of context as far as the discussion group is concerned . . . You have ripped the Catholic Action developmental plan out of context and thrust it on the group as a whole . . . That is not to accept facts, but to distort it to your own half-vision, your own selfish vision, I might say, in that your interest lies in Blessed Martin, so you direct all the group to that . . . I emphasize the idea of community so forcefully because, at whatever cost in action, I am convinced that the community, that communities, must be developed . . .

Confess up. It is your project; you are Dorothy Day, and those who wish to follow may. This would be fair and just. But do not pose yourself as a member of a community when actually you place yourself above community. This is radiantly, brilliantly clear. You could not miss my point. I only ask you to act with honor and integrity.

The project was conceived in the group, yet, you wrote to the Bishop asking for a meeting, enclosing a platform written by yourself, without the approval or consent of the group . . . probably set Catholic Action in Memphis back twenty years . . . This was not a group action, but a Helen action. This is what I mean by individualistic, selfish, dishonorable and impetuous—or at least those words hit around such an act . . . The members of the group who have been most regular and faithful were in disagreement with your presumption here and they seriously questioned your financial plans. Now, as far as numbers are concerned, surely you might have had a meeting of strangers to the work, and they all sided with you. I for one would never draw hard lines between regulars and strangers. I am only saying that you should have respected those whose judgments should be more respected, and even you must admit that some judgments are to be respected more than others. Someone told me that you had brought forth a silent group of Negro supporters. I would not presume to say that they provided you with numerical power, but such has been hinted to me; and *if*—please hinge all on the "if"—if this is where you "gained community support," I think it all despicable. This may, of course, not be the case. Please note how reserved my criticism is in this respect, since I do not know and was not there.

. . . Because the plan of the Community has momentarily lapsed into argumentation does not mean that it should be abandoned, and that you should assume leadership of a status quoism as far as the group is concerned. You simply could not plan the program in an orderly fashion, for one thing.

That is my say. I would say offhand that Joan would be the ideal organizer, working closely with you or Jane, who is new but certainly willing, and to be frank, I consider the holiest of all who have set foot in our meetings. This is a strong quality to be ignored. I do not insist that you follow my suggestions or that you defend your actions to me; I do insist that [the course suggested] should be followed *re* the St. Anthony's group.

It did not need a signature. I put the letter in my lap and laid my head down on my arms. I felt weak and drained of all emotion. In me was only the most terrible darkness. *What is the use?* I thought. What is the use of anything? Why don't you just give the whole thing up, forget it, find peace for yourself? *You can't mix the races.* The poverty you're looking for died in the Middle Ages. Forget it. Forget it. *Forget it . . .*

I kept pushing the torturing thoughts back, but they drove in on me still. Where had I been wrong? Where was the first mistake? Had there been so many by now that they were completely beyond repair? Was it really pride and selfishness that had led me here to the threshold of Blessed Martin House, to open it—instead of the Will of God, as I had believed? Had not Father Joe always distrusted my ideas and warned me against them, and others against them? Was he not right, after all, since all that he said was borne out so well by this letter from a friend?

I would not read it again because I could not.

I don't know how to describe what I felt. It was as if I had suddenly plunged from a great height into a pit of terrors unknown and hitherto unsuspected. I was so weak I could not try, nor even want to try, to save myself. I wanted only to creep away like some animal to lick its wounds. I could not bear that others should see my wretchedness. I lost all sense of proportion and of security, all confidence in the support of my friends.

What had I done? How blind, how stupid, how slow to understand could I be? How many others felt about me the way the writer of this letter felt? Father Coyne and others who might have been thinking and saying these things which my friend repeated—why had they not so much as hinted them to me? Was I really so stubbornly proud that they had not even trusted themselves to speak to me against my own ideas and wishes? But they must have known it couldn't last, that someone like me can't start a project like the one proposed. Why had they not spoken, but instead let me get so hopelessly involved that now I did not know which way to turn, to start out again? I was filled with a great shame and humiliation. And this shamed me even more, because I knew then that I was not humble, that I was proud, or these things would not have hurt so, but I could have offered them joyfully to Our Lord.

Then I tried to pray. But I could not pray—at least, not as I understood prayer. Then, least of all, could I pray. I had been following Something in trying to lead the group, in trying to plan the house. This time I was sure it was not my own will only because the closer the house came to becoming a reality, the more afraid I was, the more excuses I thought of to delay it, to postpone it; the more I wanted *not* to do it at all.

What had I followed? Then it seemed to me that a shadow fell, like that of the Prince of darkness in my mind; and I wondered if it had been he after all?

And You, my God, I kept thinking; I was trying to serve You, to please You! Where were You when I asked for guidance, for help, for wisdom and humility? Where were You when I went so blindly and stupidly along in my own path believing it Yours, thinking You were still beside me when I had long ago left You behind?

And in that terrible darkness of spirit that had come upon me, I wished so much that I might have had at least the consolation of knowing that He forgave me, that He was not too much displeased with me, that He loved me at least for my misguided efforts, and the reassurance that at least I had done my best.

But He was silent. And I felt nothing at all except an incredible weakness and weariness. I looked for Him but He would not come to me, no, not even with the sense of His Presence, of His Love.

In the next few days several more letters came, all from the same writer. They did not cause the same pain as the first because I knew before I opened them what they would contain. I read them through sadly and put them aside. I would not answer them because there seemed to to be no answer possible. There were no questions, just statements, and these backed up by the testimony of others whose sincerity and veracity seemed, even to me, unquestionable. Anything I could say, I believed, could only serve to make matters worse. So I remained silent. I did not try to answer them then.

I rallied from the first shock enough to think, with some sense of proportion, of what now must be done. In a strange kind of numbness I tried to plan.

If the accusations contained in the letters were true, one thing was certain: the house must not be. Several friends from my Catholic Worker days and Mrs. Brunner of the C.U.S.A. had sent me large donations to help towards the opening of the house. That money must be sent back. God did not want the efforts—could not be glorified possibly by the efforts—of one still so far away from Him as I was. That much seemed clear.

Much had already been done; now it would have to be undone if the letter-writer's summary of the situation were right. It seemed improbable to me that it could be wrong in the main. Some incidents the letters reported were plainly distorted, though perhaps not intentionally. But no allowance I could make for a distorted view on the part of the writer could account for the wholly different picture I had now been given of the attitude of the group. Some people whose objections were described in the letters had spoken during our meetings in a way that I had interpreted quite differently. If all the time they had actually been *thinking* in the way the letters claimed, how was I to weigh the worth of *anything* said in future meetings? Whether the unspoken (to me) opposition to the project were confined to a few or widespread was not the main issue. Doubt and suspicion would put the house just coming into being under too great a strain. Better that it should wait years, as I had intended in the beginning, than open under such circumstances, I thought. Yet I found no peace nor consolation in the thought.

Father Coyne was the moderator. He should be consulted before any action was taken, I knew. I would have to talk to him about it, and I dreaded it most terribly, since I was sure that my raising the question would force him to tell me frankly of my pride and presumption. It was hard enough to read it. I did not know if I could stand to hear it. Perhaps though, I thought, it was through this that Our Lord wanted to humble me. I could offer it in partial reparation for the faults which had occasioned it. That wasn't very much to offer. But it was all I had. I waited a few days, to gain courage, and then went to him.

"I have had several letters from a member of the study group," I began rather hesitantly. "I'm going to let you be the judge. If you think there's truth in them, please say so, and stop me before I get in any deeper than I am now."

Father Coyne looked at me, a little puzzled, then at the letters, and after a moment accepted them. "Sit down," he invited me, and took a chair for himself. Without further ado he unfolded the letters and began to read. I watched his face anxiously, trying to read it as he read.

Gradually a great red flush spread over his neck and face, and his blue eyes blazed as he put the second letter down. Father was angry. I had never seen him, nor any priest, angry before, and I was startled out of my discomfiture.

Irishmen never swear, of course, so Father Coyne, being a true Irishman, just said, "Who do they think they are?"

After that, I found it easy to talk to him about the problems the letters had presented. He did not think the letters spoke for the group. Certainly they did not speak for him, he said, and named several other members who had been with the group from its beginning as well as some new members—nor for these, he was also certain. He pushed the incidents described aside as untrue or unimportant. When I suggested that we forget the Blessed Martin House project altogether for the time being, he gave an emphatic "No."

"Well, what about the study group, about those who want a program of more concentrated study, the leadership training program, in other words? They think I have completely forsaken the leadership training program and substituted the Blessed Martin House project for my own selfish ends because that is where my interest lies. They also seemed pretty much agreed, judging from the letters, that I am incapable of leading the other program anyway."

"Sure, you couldn't lead it like Jim," Father admitted. "But Jim is not here. It has to be developed by and with the people here. I don't have time to plan the kind of program Jim had in mind, and frankly I don't know anybody in the study group who is capable of doing it, and who would take the responsibility for it. I think we should go on with the Blessed Martin House project and let the group decide whether they want to follow you or not."

"You mean you want me to present the problem to the group?"

"No, I think it would be better if I did it. I can explain

that there has been some misunderstanding about the house and the leadership training program and about the question of leadership and of a moderator for the other part of the program. Then they can choose."

"Do you think I should answer the letters? I have not. It seems to me it would be useless for me to try to explain anything now when they have already made up their minds anyway as to what has happened. I don't think I should try to explain or justify myself under those circumstances, do you?"

"Maybe you should not," he agreed. "Probably silence is the best defense for you. But I am going to answer myself, I have something to say."

At our next meeting of the study group, Father presented the problem. The group had definitely decided on two aims before Jim left, he said: (1) the Blessed Martin House project, and (2) the leadership training program. The two were complements, each necessary to the other. The Blessed Martin House was to be an adjunct, so to speak, independent, but affiliated, a place where the leadership training group could act or practice. The leadership training program would be the future of the existing group, as far as prayer and study were concerned. It was to become, to a greater extent, conducted through diocesan direction, and we had gone to see the diocesan priests concerning it, and they had sent us back to him. That was where it had stood when Jim left.

"Now," Father Coyne explained, "we have been able to develop the Blessed Martin House project, with the blessing of our Bishop, and are ready to start. The interest of most members of the group has been so concentrated on this program that we agreed as a group to concentrate on it principally for a while, and Helen agreed to direct the

Blessed Martin House, to live there herself, to dedicate herself, in a way of speaking, to that work, if the house came into being. Therefore we have not been much concerned lately with the leadership training program. Besides this, no leader has come forth for it, since Jim has gone, and I cannot lead it, and there are those who do not feel Helen should lead it. Because there has been this misunderstanding I feel that we should decide as a group what should be our principal aim, the Blessed Martin House or the leadership training program."

Almost all of the group decided on the house, because "study, prayer and discussion can be carried on at the house as a part of it. It's in the platform which the Bishop approved. But the leadership training program without some definite basis to hold it together, more than study of the kind we could devote to it, would probably fall to pieces in a little while. We can see that in the turnover in this group and in the collapse of study groups in other parishes and places. We think the house is most important. Besides, our Bishop thinks of the house the same way. That should count the most for it," one member summed it up.

So the group decided to make the support of the Blessed Martin House the chief aim of its existence, with study, prayer, and discussion a part of the Blessed Martin House program; moreover, a part at least as important as the corporal works of mercy dispensed by the house.

Father asked then if the group were willing to follow or back up my ideas as to the meaning, aim and method of the house as expressed in its platform, particularly in regard to race, poverty, location, support, and so on, with the other things so much debated.

"She's the one who's got to live there," one member,

the newspaperman, remarked. "If she's willing to give up her job and live there, on duty, as it were, twenty-four hours a day, depending only on the Providence of God to support her, I say more power to her! If she's got that much faith and nerve, or whatever it takes, my wife and I will help her all we can."

This was seconded and approved by most, so Father Coyne said, "That's it, then. Our chief interest will be in Blessed Martin House: we will all, each in his own way, help her as much as we can."

"What about the leadership training program?" Joan wanted to know.

"I think we should just drop it as such, for right now," someone said. "There is no one to lead it."

"But we will have a study program at Blessed Martin House, as a part of the work of the house, that could be about the same thing," I said. "I could not lead the other program now. If there are those who are especially interested in that, maybe they can work out a program together, and you can use the house as a sort of headquarters. It should be developed. I'll help all I can if you want me to."

"I don't think I could direct the kind of program Jim always had in mind," Father Coyne said again. "That would take a lot of study and planning and time. I don't have the time for it. Besides, I think Jim was right when he said a diocesan priest would probably be better for that sort of program, to reach the white as well as the colored parishes. Then too, there is the problem of a leader. Who would lead the program?

No one volunteered, so I asked, in turn, some of those who had been suggested to me as leaders, but none would accept. The meeting closed on that. In the future, the Blessed Martin House would be our main end as a group, and the leadership training program as such was to take a long rest, but Blessed Martin House itself would have a program of discussion and study for all those who were interested in it. This would be called the "Outer Circle," and the members obliged themselves to support those parts of the Blessed Martin House program with which they were in agreement. It was not necessary that all members of the Outer Circle accept and believe every single one of the Blessed Martin House principles, nor could the members be legally held responsible for debts contracted by the house, nor infractions of law (we were thinking of the racial laws which we intended at times to ignore) on the part of the house; nor could they be held accountable as members for any stand the house might take on wages, labor, race, etc. At the same time, they would act as volunteers, *helpers,* to the house and not as directors, advising and suggesting but not deciding. Father Coyne, as spiritual director, was excepted, of course, and could have the final say on anything which threatened the spiritual welfare of the house, and since practically anything of importance might justly be said to help or threaten that, it did leave a certain balance and safeguard over my own actions.

After this, I still received a few other letters but the tone of them changed. One said: "Really, now what do you take me for? I use the word Negro as a descriptive adjective and you expand it into an awesome backhanded slap at your race . . . what I meant was that you were deriving much of your strength in the group from a group of new members brought in by you who are Negroes . . . the Negro was solely for identification."

I should have known. But I did not know. Too much had happened all at once. I could not know anything.

Another said, "I'm glad there will be a Blessed Martin

House. If I can help, let me know. Were I in the same situation again, I would probably act hastily again, risking clarity for the sake of the big intention . . . I would do everything in my power to help—materials, labor, soliciting, finances. I can criticize (which I hope is constructive); and I can pray. I can suggest ways and means."

That made a lot of difference, and I felt better on that score. I had not lost a friend after all, and the group for the most part wanted the house. Thank God for that much, I thought.

12

Even though father coyne's talk to the members of the group had settled the questions and doubts of others, and helped me tremendously, it had not settled the questions and doubts in my own mind. They had been there before, down deep, hidden; now the letters had brought them up to light, and nothing Father said quite touched the source of my anxiety. Perhaps it was that he was so close to the situation that I was afraid to trust his judgment.

Then there was the opposition at home, expected but nonetheless trying and painful.

"You can go on with this insanity if you want, for yourself," Don told me, "but you aren't going to take the Old Man" (Butch) "with you down to that rat-hole. If you want to throw your own life away for a bunch of pimps and prostitutes, that's your business, but the Old Man deserves something better. You owe it to him to give him a good home and try to make him happy. He has a right to the kind of life you can give him now with your writing and your nursing. If you couldn't do any better, it would be a different thing; I wouldn't say a word. With all the brains you have, I don't see how you can be so stupid!"

"I'm not throwing my life away for drunks and prostitutes," I said, "I'm trying to live in what seems to me a more perfect way and give Butch that security, which seems to me more important than the one I could give him if I did it your way, with material things. How can I explain it to you, or how can you expect to understand it, when you don't even believe in God? What I expect to get in return, and expect for Butch, is not something I can put in words you could understand. But it's real just the same, just as real as anything more tangible I might be taking from him."

"Don't tell me anything about it," he said. "You may know everything else; I know that neighborhood. Right down there in that very place you're thinking of renting, I was delivering whiskey one day a few years back and found a dead woman. She had been murdered and left there for days before anybody even found her. I can see that some people get their happiness or pleasure in doing this and some in doing the other, and that's all right. But you've got to think of Butch."

"It's not a question of my happiness or pleasure," I pleaded, "but a question of doing what pleases God."

"God!" He sneered. "In every age people have been cut and burned and beaten and killed in the name of God. I have one God. I can hold him in my pocket, and when he talks, everybody listens." He waved a bill under my nose. "You think you can change people by talking, showing them? You want to make white people black and black people white. It will never happen. The white man is tops now, always was, and always will be. This is the only thing that can change it, even a little bit. Money. Power."

117

"You can't eat it."

"Yeah, but it will buy a whole lot of food. More than your lectures and talks and discussions."

"It won't buy the only food I want to feed on and want Butch to have. It won't buy love and it won't buy heaven."

"Show me first there is a heaven," he suggested.

My brothers were no less vehement in their opposition.

"You've got to think of yourself," Junior argued. "You haven't been out of the hospital two years. You still go to the doctor for treatment every week. And you want to go down there in that filthy rat-hole and live in poverty," he mocked, "You haven't enough of poverty, and fighting. You've just spent a few good years of your life learning to do something, to have and be something, and now you are going to throw it away just like that? You said you wanted to be a nurse and a writer, and Mother and all of us helped and encouraged you. You say you love your work and your patients. Why can't you be satisfied with that, then? Why do you want to do something crazy, that doesn't make much sense to anybody but you? Can't you help the poor just as much, as a nurse in the hospital, as you can down on Beale Street taking care of somebody's children? And what about your own child? Who is going to take care of him if something happens to you down there? You have to think of those things too, you know."

"Besides," William, my younger brother, pointed out, "I'm still in school and Junior has a big family, four children. Neither of us could help Mother very much right now if some emergency came up. It's your duty to help her out until we are able to."

"Now don't you worry about me," Mother said when

she heard this. (Except for my father, who was a little better than neutral, she was the only one who defended me.) "I will be all right. If that is what she wants to do, I don't think we ought to discourage her. Somebody has to take care of those no one else cares or thinks about. Don't worry about me. I'll be all right. Don has done all right so far, and I haven't had to come to any of you very much for help."

"And," I said, "as far as emergencies are concerned, who would take care of them if I were still in the hospital, as I well might be, or if I had to go back, as I well might do, even if I continue working as a nurse? Just remember that it was as a nurse working under the most hygienic conditions possible that I contracted T.B. in the first place. So it's no use in you all talking about 'filthy rat-holes.' Sure it's dirty, but there's no dirt there a little soap and water and disinfectant can't control. We can spend our whole lives trembling and afraid, so far as that goes, for an emergency that never comes. We have to trust God in something. If I give to Him generously, I don't think He will return stingily. He is not going to let me be more generous than He is Himself. I'm not afraid of that part. If I take care of every day. He can handle the emergencies. In the end, He always does, anyway."

"Well, it's your own funeral," they both told me. "We sure hope you won't be sorry, but we are mighty afraid you will be. The world and people are not like you think they are. But you will see. Experience is a dear teacher, as Daddy says, and fools will learn by no other."

As for Daddy himself, he said little, he was leaving it up to me. He didn't understand, but he could see some possibility of good and he admitted that there certainly was a need for some such place as Blessed Martin House was going to be. "You can do a lot by teaching and example in a place like that," he said.

He meant, of course, with regard to temporal things and good social habits in the community—habits of health, hygiene, moral (natural) character, and so on. But that much *meant* more, coming from him. He asked me to let him know if he could be of help.

But the family objections were not the hardest part. The hardest part was myself. Suppose I was being selfish and presumptuous? Suppose I was being unfair to my child? Suppose the whole thing was not God's will but my own? Suppose I was incapable of carrying it out and it became a scandal to others, so they could say: "She trusted in God and God failed her," and lost faith because of me?

I sat down at last and wrote to my dear friends and beloved counselors, Fathers Meenan and Kirby, explaining the situation and asking their advice. I talked it over with my confessor and asked his advice. I showed him the letters which had caused so much turmoil.

He did not know enough of the situation in the light of that information, he said, to judge, but in the light of our moderator's and the Bishop's decision, he would say go ahead with the project. He did not know if I were capable or not, time would have to tell. As for Butch, he certainly was my chief responsibility, and I should weigh well the things I would take from him by bringing him up in this apostolate, against the things he gained by it.

He agreed that being brought up in an atmosphere that breathed Christ, in love and dependence on God, which ignored race and prejudice and helped others to do so and to live more fully or more joyously in spirit, or more comfortably in body and mind, might well outweigh the material comforts that I might give Butch by sticking to a more orthodox way of life. The decision was mine to make, however, he said.

I reread a letter I had received from Father Kirby not long before. And I took courage from the things he said: "Remember too that works that have clear sailing and no opposition in the beginning are usually short-lived. Those that sometimes get beaten into the ground by opposition spring up to live forever; they are not dead, they are only digging in, striking roots in the heart of the Savior, the eternal spring.

"God wants us to do our humble, quiet best. 'Learn of Me,' He said, 'for I am meek and humble of heart.' That is where our big struggle is, right in our own heart."

But it was Father Meenan's letter that really decided me. With his wonderful insight he reached at once the heart of the problem and explained it simply to me. I understood then and I was not afraid any more.

"I am rereading your letter," he wrote, "for the second or third time, and now I am going to begin an answer. The first question we meet is this: Is the present plan your will or God's will? The angels won't tell you, but the Bishop and the priest appointed by him say 'Go ahead.' That means that it is God's will that you try. If He does not want it, it will never succeed; if He does want it, it will never fail. As for yourself, never fear, never despair, even in the blackest moments; results are God's business, and He will attend to them. Lay the whole matter at His feet each day to do with as He sees fit, then just go to work and do your best.

"Next, as regards your lack of ability or capacity to

lead. That is merely a part of the above situation. You probably are quite incapable, and quite stupid in disregarding material guarantees of success and respectability. Hence you will never have any reason to take credit for any success that Providence may work through you. Ever since God started a world Church with twelve fishermen, He has been picking the most incapable people, it seems, to do things He wants done. Remember always this, lack of ability, of talents, is no hindrance to God's plan. Only one thing can hinder it, lack of sanctity, of sincere and efficacious desire to strive for it, in the people He chooses to do His work. So on score number two, I would give you another green light."

Then followed a list of good and practical suggestions concerning the house, concerning method and policy. He ended: "Finally, as regards yourself and Butch, he is your first obligation, and no other calling can be permitted to deprive him of the love and care that only you can give. Do not underestimate the importance of your physical presence as well as your providing for his spiritual and physical needs.

"God love you and give you the grace to suffer much for Him."

The last of my doubts was gone. One of the principal works of the house was the nursery, so in the house, as in no other work, could I give my time to Butch, even while working to provide for those other needs. I would not have to leave him and "go to work," as I had been doing; he too was now a part of the work. If God provided for the work to continue, Butch would benefit rather than lose. I was not taking anything important from him but was giving him something far more important, my love, my presence, my care, my instruction, and the *security* of depending on the greatest and most indulgent of Fathers.

"If your son ask for bread, will you give him a stone?" Why had I been afraid? God loved Butch at least as much as I did. At last I was at peace. I knew I would open Blessed Martin House.

13

It took about two months to fix up the place for Blessed Martin House, just to make it barely habitable; two months of prodding the unwilling landlord into repairing the worst portions of the rotten flooring and the biggest holes in the wall and ceiling, fixing knobs on doors and making screen doors. He would not paint the interior nor really clean it, even though we had paid a month's advance on the seventy-five dollars a month rent. Neither would he move the giant electric soda fountain, which wouldn't work and was in the way. He claimed he had no place to store it, so we had to clean around and under the monstrosity.

Only a few members of the group would come down and help clean and fix up the place, because it seemed to them so impossible that it could ever look livable. Of course, some really did not have time, especially the mothers of families. I tried to get my brothers, who were at home, to come and help, but they still strongly disapproved of the project. William did come for a few hours; then Junior came and talked to him, and he wouldn't come back any more. I guess they were trying to make it so hard for me that I would have to give it up.

Several people in Memphis gave furniture, dishes or money, mostly members of the group or their friends, but in the beginning, the greatest part of the financial support came from friends outside Memphis.

Mary Smith and her husband helped me lay the linoleum for the floor (he did most of the work), and Mr. Smith fixed up several other needed things as well. Several of the members of the group who were students helped paint the tables and chairs, and Father Coyne talked to the students at St. Anthony's and persuaded two high school boys to help me with the painting of the front outside wall. I found some colorful plastic curtains downtown for the windows, and someone helped me to hang them.

These improvements made the place look so much better that others volunteered to help as they began to see the possibilities. The neighborhood children came in to watch and often stayed to help, especially Mary Lou, Mary Lee and Catherine. Dan, Catherine's cousin, ran errands, and even Delia, a chronic alcoholic who lived upstairs, came with the intention of helping—really she was more in the way. She was really proud of the place, always bragging about it and bringing her friends to see it. She assured Father Coyne of her love for Catholics, especially priests, and was forever embarrassing or shaming me by her extravagant praise. A thin old man with a face like a skeleton, who lived nearby, also came to help a lot, and of course, Butch and Mother.

Butch and I painted our room—there were two rooms, one wide one that had been a cafe and one tiny one that had probably been a storeroom. This had no windows but a small glass in its door. Butch painted as far as he could reach, and I painted all above him, going over his streaky places too. Mother kept a warm meal waiting at home and laundered things for us and for the house, and when the time came, she and Rosemary helped me arrange the furniture. Rosemary's husband had a truck, and he picked up and delivered things for us and lifted the heavy things we had to move. Father Coyne helped with things like that too. The sisters at St. Anthony's made a beautiful sign to hang at the door—"Blessed Martin House of Hospitality".

At last everything was ready. The outside front was painted blue, our Lady's color, in her honor. The sign was hung directly under the door-light. The windows were clean and shining. Inside there were bright curtains, and pretty spreads for the baby beds, and colorful covers for the couches. There were toys for the children to play with, bright chairs on which they could sit. One table was for eating; that had a cloth; the others were for play, and so were uncovered but pretty in their new paint. Pictures were hung from the walls here and there. Our Lady of Guadaloupe, Our Lady of Perpetual Help, a varnished icon of Ss. Peter and Paul and, dearest of all to me, a beautiful "Black Madonna," Our Lady, Queen of Poland, which Father Jarzembowski had sent. Book cases were along the walls, and on one stood a small statue of Blessed Martin de Porres, which was the gift of the sisters at St. Augustine's.

At last we were finished, and Butch and I moved in. Mother had fixed a nice hot dinner for us, string beans and Irish potatoes, some meat and dessert. I set the table that night, and for the first time Butch and I said grace together in our new "home." At the last moment we discovered that we had beautiful dishes and glasses but no forks or spoons, so we laughingly ate with our fingers.

After supper I read Butch a story and then took him on my lap to sing to him. He liked to have me make up songs for him, and I often did. His favorites were "St. Francis" and "Hiawatha". I mostly made them to the tune of a familiar folk song (the songs I sang for him which I did not make were usually folk songs). These two were based on "O Sole Mio" and a real song about Hiawatha from a little operetta, both tunes somewhat modified.

"What do you want Mother to sing?" I asked him.

"Sing about St. Francis."

"All right, because now we are going to live a little like St. Francis, St. Francis and Blessed Martin."

"Do you know a song about Blessed Martin?"

"No, Mother will have to make you one about him another day. Mother is tired tonight."

"Then sing about St. Francis."

"Okay." And I began to sing the song (but the lines in italics I always spoke, never sang):

> In a little town
> That was called Assisi
> There lived a man
> Whose name was Francis
> And he loved God
> How he loved God!
> And all the creatures
> Which God had made.
>
> Now in a town
> That was near Assisi

There lived a big wolf
An ugly big wolf
And he would eat
The townsmen's sheep up
And little chickens
And baby lambs

Yes, he would eat
The townsmen's cows up
And little ducklin's
And kitty cats too.
Yes, he would eat
The townsmen's puppies
And little chickens
And kitty cats.

So all the townsmen
They got their guns out
To shoot that big wolf
And kill that big wolf.
They chased and chased him
Over hill and valley
And wind-swept prairie
And grassy lanes.

But then St. Francis
He said unto them:
"Oh, no, good townsmen
Oh, no, no, no, no!
Don't chase that big wolf
Don't hurt that big wolf
Don't shoot that big wolf
Don't kill the wolf."

And then St. Francis
He said unto him:

"Brother Wolf, Brother Wolf!
Come here to me!___
What d'you do it for, Huh?
Why'd you eat the townsmen's sheep
And baby lambs and little ducks
And kitty cats and things?"

And then that big wolf
Went to St. Francis
And put his big paw
In Francis' hand there.
He hung his head
To show his shame
And put his big paw
In Francis' hand
As if to say:

"I'm sorry. I didn't mean to do it.
I was hungry. And nobody wouldn't
Give me nothin to eat.
So I just ate the cows and
Chickens and things.
I'm sorry. I won't do it no more.
But don't let the men shoot me.
I'll be real, real good."

And so St. Francis
He said unto him:
"Then promise me, wolf
Then promise me now

That you won't eat
The townsmen's sheep up
Or little ducklings
Or other things.

"And I will promise
That all the townsmen
Will treat you kindly
Just like a puppy.
They'll give meat to eat
And give you bones to eat
And pet you fondly
Just like a dog."

And so they promised
The good St. Francis
And that great big wolf.
They sealed their promise
And they did sing
Did sing together:
"Praise be to God!
Praise be to God!"

When the song was finished I began undressing Butch
for bed. I was there, that was enough for him. He was
happy and unafraid. But I was a little fearful—to be alone,
with only him for company, at night in a strange neighborhood. I tested the doors and made certain that the telephone was in easy reach of my hand. Then I knelt down
with Butch to help him say his prayers.

"Hail Mary," that was first; then the "blesses," and
last "I'm sorry if I've been a bad boy today, help me to
be good. I offer everything that hurt me for the Glory
of God and the conversion of sinners. Amen."

I finished my own prayers and climbed into bed with

him. He had a little bed of his own, but this first night I would sleep with him, lest he wake up feeling frightened and alone in a strange place.

A few days later, on the feast of the Epiphany, January 6, we had our official opening. Most of the study group was there, and Father Robert, the pastor of St. Bridget's, the church we attended on the corner a block away. Father Murphy was there from Sacred Heart. I had met him while I was working as a nurse. I had gone to church at Sacred Heart because it was nearest to the hospital. One day he had come to see me at the hospital to tell me that he had read and enjoyed my book. I had told him about the study group, and later, when the new program of study was made up, invited him to speak and lead one of the discussions. He had accepted, and we had become fast friends. I learned that he had worked with Friendship House for a little while when he was a seminarian and that he had a great love for the lay apostolate and great faith in it. Father Coyne was there too, of course, and a new colored member of the study group, Gladys Kinkle.

We had a little party, and Father Coyne spoke to us, and so did Father Murphy. Everyone who was not already possessed of one, received a mimeographed copy of our study program for the next few months.

Blessed Martin House
(Outer Circle Study Plan)
Thursday, January 10, 1952
    8:00 P.M. Father Murphy: "The Soul of the Apostolate"
    8:30 P.M. Questions and Answers Period
    9:00 P.M. Specific Problems of the House
Thursday, January 24, 1952
    Alice Hanrahan: "The Spirit of Poverty"

Thursday, February 7, 1952
   Phyllis O'Callaghan: "Charity and Mutual Aid in the
      Apostolate"
Thursday, February 28, 1952
   Dot Wells: "Some Problems of the Apostolate"
Thursday, February 28, 1952.
   Father Wiley: "The Need for Spiritual Direction"

The other topics of discussion up to April 22 were also listed, but I had not yet found speakers for them.

There were coffee and cookies afterwards, and general conversation. Everyone was surprised to see what had been done to the house. But I treasured most what Father Murphy said; "It looks like a real Friendship House." I knew that was a great compliment from him.

I knew how much he admired Friendship House and knew he meant that we had tried to make much from almost nothing—and succeeded. There was an atmosphere of simplicity, warmth, and cheer in this room of the ugly old building that somehow set it apart from the drabness and wretchedness of its surroundings. It was as if the blessing which Father Coyne had given it had taken visible form to make beautiful the cheap and tawdry.

At last everyone had gone and Butch and I were alone again. Butch had long since fallen asleep. I undressed and put him to bed, then kneeled a few moments in prayer and went to bed myself. Tomorrow the work would begin.

The next day the first children began to come. James, Jovita, Elizabeth and Dan. All were around two years old, except Dan, who was around Butch's age, five or six.

Butch played with them and did not seem to mind the attention I had to give the babies. In fact, he would call my attention to a need: "Mother, this baby wet on the floor."

He wanted to help me feed them. I let him try but the babies didn't like that, so I took over the job.

In the evening after school, groups of neighborhood children, most between six and twelve, came in to play games. A number of teen-age boys came too, including one white boy, and when I was ready to close each night, one or two would stay to help me clean up.

I asked the mothers of the children in the nursery to help with the work of the house sometimes, but it was not yet a rule because the children in the nursery were still so few and the house so new.

The larger children at that time were the ones who enjoyed the greatest benefits from the house, so they had the responsibility, within their capacities, of keeping it nice for themselves.

As news of the house's activities spread by word of mouth and, in the beginning, through the local newspaper and colored radio station, more children began to come into the nursery, and the responsibilities of the mothers grew, while that of the school children decreased. The mothers took turns coming once a week for a few hours to take care of, or help take care of, the house and supervise the children. They also checked in and out books from the library. Still, the school children had their responsibilities too. Some were "police," delegated to keep order and prevent cheating. They had the authority to put another child outside if, after repeated warning, the child refused to cooperate, or persisted in some act of mischief, or started a fight. The child thus "evicted" could appeal to me, but the issue was finally settled in "court" every Friday evening by a jury and judge made up of the children themselves. Every Saturday night we had a party and there was a little treat—candy, nuts, and occasionally ice cream, which had been donated. Sometimes Father Coyne came down to show a free movie.

People began to send us used clothing, some very good, and I would call aside some of the children whose dress betrayed their need and offer to give them clothes if their mothers consented. Most did, so clothing was distributed in this way. Many brought back small sisters and brothers or neighbors' children, and when I was convinced the need was genuine, these also received clothing.

By spring the number of children in the nursery had grown to about fifteen or sixteen and the older children were still coming at night and to the Outer Circle meeting every two weeks. I had almost no help except from the children and a few of the mothers who came a few hours each week and really pitched in to work. Some of the mothers made excuses and never came to help. After talking this over with Father Coyne, I decided to have a mothers' meeting once a month to help them to understand why we had the house and what their own place was in it. We also decided to make it a rule, in general, that all mothers who left children in the nursery must come to help with the work of the house one day a week. However, because I had seen, and we knew, that there were women in neighborhoods like this who habitually left their children alone, or in irresponsible hands, we readily make exceptions to this rule, for the sake of the children who needed care. Thus it was that mothers were strongly encouraged to help at the house, but until I knew them well enough to be sure of their love and mature sense of responsibility toward their children, they were not really put under great pressure to do so if they seemed unwilling. It seems, at first glance, a casual and careless way of making rules and dealing with people, and some members of the Outer Circle and others thought it encouraged irresponsibility in parents.

There is, admittedly, danger there, as there is danger in living and loving. We just have to be aware of the dangers and try to work around them. For I don't think those people who made this criticism have gone into a tenement, as I have, to bring a baby to "my" house to care for him because his mother was leaving him every day in the care of a five-year-old child, asking a habitually drunken neighbor to "look in on them every now and then." (This woman lived close to the nursery, knew about the nursery, but would not come to it because she was unwilling to help once a week or to feel "under obligation." Rather than that, she would leave her baby as I have described.) They have not seen families of six or eight children crowded in one room with a mother with the intelligence of a child.

What, then? Should I have let the children suffer? Should I have refused to take them? "Whatsoever you have done to the least of these," Our Lord said, "you have done it unto Me." "Whoever receives such a little child in my name, receives Me." "A new commandment I give you, that you love one another as I have loved you."

What did I know of the life and suffering of this woman who so neglected her baby, that had made her so unfeeling or so unthinking? I knew she shared her bed with others than her husband. How many? I don't know. She was poor in everything, morally, materially, physically, mentally, spiritually. Hers was an open life of sin, but if mine were not, was it due to my own strength or God's grace? I knew it was not my own strength, because I know my own sins. If they have been less obvious, they have not been less great. Or that woman who did not know the fathers of her babies, what did I know of her mentality or her temptations?

No, Our Lord said, "Judge not," and least of all would I presume to judge them. I would rather love and work to bring down God's mercy in love. And even if I could judge them, there were the children to be considered, their innocence and their need.

Therefore, even though it was, to some, a scandal, we took the children, cared for them daily. If necessary we fed and clothed them daily too, without insisting on any human return, not even help, love, or gratitude. We still do, because we want to follow the example of Our Lord, who "makes the rain to fall on the just and the unjust," and the sun to shine and the grass to grow, for them as well as for His saints.

Each family posed its own individual problem, and the idea of Blessed Martin House is the idea of personal responsibility for individual needs. If there is reason to believe that strictness, severity, or firmness is the best way to reach this person and help her grow, that is the method we use. For some there are the rules in the house, almost inflexible. For some there is only (what seems to others) a timid, fearful love that gives in and backs down, and bends over as if there were no rules at all. But again, it is to help each person to grow and become the great person God intended her to be.

There is every approach in between, and always the prayer that God will help us use the right one. For the poorest and most forsaken, the Godless and forgotten, always it is the way of mercy, of giving in, waiting, taking, swallowing words of just anger, being patient and trying to see Christ, who comes to us through these, His least brethren.

14

Blessed Martin House was four or five months old when Mary St. Onge came to visit from Nashville. She called first to say she wanted to come, and I said "Come on." However, I warned her, as I am careful to warn all would-be white overnight guests, of the possibility of arrest, of fine or even jail for us if anyone wanted to be nasty. White and colored are forbidden by law to stay overnight under the same roof unless the colored person is staying as a servant. Only a few years ago in the papers there was the report of a white preacher jailed and fined for this "offense" in Memphis. He had no place to go and accepted the Christian hospitality of a Negro friend. So he was a criminal. He was lectured and had to pay a fine.

But Mary was willing to take the risk, as I was. We believe that one must live according to one's beliefs; and that to deny Christ in His brethren is to deny Christ in Himself. The state may make laws, if it will, and I will obey them as far as my conscience permits. But no law but God's can compel my conscience, His law in His scripture, tradition, or in His Church. And I think she felt the same. It was such laws as these that made Christians martyrs in the early days of the Church, because they refused to render to Caesar the things that are God's.

Mary came. She remained with me for several days, helping at the house, meeting and talking to the members of the Outer Circle study group. She had been inspired by the interracial apostolate of Friendship House and had opened a community center for Negro children in Nashville. They had a girls' basketball team and several other activities. She did not have many teen-agers in her group, she told me, and she seemed very surprised to find so many at Blessed Martin House, especially teen-age boys.

I said, "That may be just as well for you, and the boys, too. You don't know what prejudice can mean down here. You are young and pretty, and if you had a group of teen-age colored boys around, somebody would start getting ideas about the boys. You might end up with a lynching or a race riot on your hands."

"Oh, I know what prejudice is, all right," she objected, and went on to tell me some of the trouble it had already caused at her house. "Still, you might be right about that. I had never thought about it in just that way. But let me tell you what has already happened."

The police had accused her of being a Communist and an agitator, she told me. They had searched her house without a warrant and subtly threatened her if she did not cease her interracial activities. White men had followed her home from church, and when they had found what she was doing, that she was living and working among Negroes, for love, they had tried to make her as uncomfortable and fearful as possible. She was all alone too, in all this, and only a youngster herself. I don't think she was as old as I, and I was twenty-five.

We talked and talked about both our houses, between working and playing. On Sunday we went fishing and hiking and practiced shooting cans with a rifle off a stick. We waded in the stream and talked and rested, and talked. We discovered that we had many things in common and knew it would be easy for us to form a genuine and warm friendship.

She wanted a person, especially a colored person, to come and live and work with her in Nashville. I wanted a white person to do the same with me in Memphis. We tried to win each other, but could not. The main reason we could not was because she wanted to, and had already started to, work on the lines of the Friendship House ideal with its accent on social justice and interracial justice, and I wanted, and had already started, to work according to the pattern of the Catholic Worker movement, of which race is only one part. The two movements are in many ways very much alike and certainly do a lot to help each other. But there is a difference, and to both of us it was too important a difference for a union to be possible. So we agreed to help and encourage each other and to visit each other, but to keep our separate houses. We parted friends, and I certainly hated to see her go. For a few days I had been free of that terrible loneliness which had nothing to do with how many people were around. Now it came back, worse than ever.

Shortly after Mary had gone, I received an invitation from a former member of our study group to go to Fort Worth, Texas, to speak about the house. I had never made any speeches except those made in classrooms in college and high school, unless you could call my contributions to the meetings of our study group "speeches" (and some did), but I accepted.

The sodality sent my fare, and soon Butch and I were on our way. (He did not have to pay.) In Fort Worth we were received very graciously and taken to a house where we could rest and spend the night. It was the home of a charming colored family, and they made us feel most welcome.

That evening we went to the school and I talked. I talked about the house in Memphis and why it came to be. I explained Peter Maurin's reasons why we need Houses of Hospitality: "to give the rich an opportunity to serve the poor, to make workers of scholars and scholars of workers, to bring Bishops to the people and people to the Bishops, to restore to institutions the technique of institutions, as places where Catholic thought could be exercised in Catholic institutions." I explained the manner in which we tried to apply these principles at Blessed Martin House, by the free nursery and library, the community center and the study group, by giving out food and clothing to those who came in need, and by attempting to find jobs for those able and willing to work. "I need help of all kinds," I ended, "but especially I need someone to work with me."

Afterwards the group clapped, and a few asked questions and seemed enthusiastic, but I don't think it made any real impression on very many, because after we returned we never heard any more from members of that group, except those who had invited us down. But anyway a seed was planted.

Shortly after that, I was invited to New Orleans to talk about the house at Caritas. Since this was another lay group, active in the apostolate, I accepted again, with enthusiasm. I had heard a lot about this work from people who were friends of both our house and theirs and had read something about the group in *Integrity* magazine. They set a date and sent train fare, so once more Butch and I were on our way. As before, Mother and Ida, the woman who lived across the street and was always so helpful, kept the house going while I was away, so I didn't have to worry about that.

In New Orleans, Dr. Bertha McGrauer, who had started the work there, and her associates, Mary Linda Hronick, Marcella Muhl, and Kathleen, met us at the station and gave us a warm welcome. Bertha drove us home to Caritas, explaining more about their work on the way.

They lived and worked in a middle-class colored neighborhood and (like Mary St. Onge) were very anxious to find a colored co-worker to make their house complete, since all were white. This, they felt, would really make them in fact, and in the sight of all, a part of the people around them. "We are parish workers in the colored parish in which we live," Bertha explained, "and we do whatever our pastor feels is most necessary. At present, we teach catechism to the public school children, because that is what he thinks is most needed. There are five hundred Catholic children who are not receiving religious instruction and we are trying to reach them."

"I'm looking for a helper too," I replied. "I'd like to have a white person, but I don't care too much if she's black, white, or green. Just so I got someone." They all laughed at this.

Mary Linda began explaining about the religious day camp which they conducted during the summer for these children, and as they described the arts and crafts, as well as religious instruction which they were able to give the children, I longed to know more and felt almost a tinge of envy because I had so little and knew so little to give and teach my children at Blessed Martin House.

"Maybe next summer you can come to our summer camp," Bertha ended. I hoped I could, and promised that I would come if possible. I did want to learn more things to teach the children at Blessed Martin House.

When we reached the house, Butch and I rested a little while, and Bertha and Mary Linda told me more about Caritas and I told them more about Blessed Martin House.

Their work had not had smooth sailing either. In New Orleans, it seemed, and all of Louisiana, white Catholics were even more prejudiced than those in Nashville and Memphis. Until recently in most, and stubbornly still in some white churches, there were signs for Negroes, telling them to take the rear seats only, and Negro communicants had to wait until white communions were finished before approaching the altar, despite the Bishop's admonitions.

I said, "Thank God, things have never been, to my knowledge, that bad in Memphis." I expressed surprise that a state with so many more Catholics than Tennessee should be so much less Catholic.

I told her how friendly I had found the people in Memphis Catholic churches. I had just been received as a postulant in the Third Order of St. Dominic at one of the white churches and had admittedly felt some trepidation at the thought of going to my first meeting alone. I had learned to love my patron, Martin de Porres, and wanted to follow him even into the third order, as well as share his humiliation in being the wrong color and belonging to the wrong race. He must have known too, and felt, I thought, the terrible loneliness of being different. But his love had been greater than his pride, and so I wanted my own to be. I asked to be received, was received, and went to the first meeting after my reception with a fearful heart and a prayer for humility and charity. But I need not have feared, for the tertiaries went out of their way to be friendly and to make me feel welcome. And after that I went with joy, glad to be child of Dominic and sister to Martin.

Bertha and Mary were surprised at this. But they were even more surprised when I told them that just as they had become a part of a colored parish and were working and living in it, taking part in its activities, so at Blessed Martin House we had become a part of the white parish in which we lived. The priest was friendly and helpful and the parishioners, as far as I could see, were at worst indifferent. I did not try to attend any strictly social affairs, but I had the excuse of being too busy. However, I did sing the Mass with the children, and I used the rectory yard as a playground for my children. When I had a problem I went without hesitation to the pastor, and he always was friendly and helpful, as becomes the shepherd of souls.

Then Kathleen told me how difficult it had been for them to find a place to live in the parish. Bertha told how their first landlord had overcharged and cheated them, knowing their desire to work and live among Negroes and knowing that few others would rent to them at all. When at last they sought and received help through the O.P.A. price control board, the landlord began throwing garbage on their porch, playing the radio loudly and banging on the walls at night, and doing other such things to disturb them. His wife circulated a petition among the neighbors against them for disturbing the peace (with interracial meetings), and once the police came down and threatened to arrest everyone if they found a "nigger" on the premises. I don't remember whether the group had dispersed by then, or whether the police simply didn't carry out their threat, but no actual arrest was made.

When these annoyances had become dangerous (one night the man shot a gun through the house) Bertha went to the police. But the officer simply pointed out that she was entitled to the protection due a white person under the law only if she *behaved like a white person*. If she insisted upon living and working among Negroes and sharing their lives, she would be treated as one. The police would not help her. She couldn't change the South, he warned her. She ought to leave it or to conform. So she had to go home with no more than that.

At last she was able to find another place to live, and they had moved. They couldn't stay in the next place long either, but soon had to move again. They had been in their present house on Green Street for some time now.

They were not discouraged, however. And that gave me courage. I laughed when Bertha repeated a story about herself. The incident had occurred when she sat in the rear of a bus with the colored, again to share our lot.

Another white woman had complained to the driver and he had come back to Bertha and asked, "Are you sure you are in the right place?"

"Oh, yes," she had assured him, and he had seemed satisfied. But the other woman was not, so he had come and asked it again. She had replied as before, explaining this time, "I have colored blood—" and had added, under her breath, as he turned his back, "It's red."

His neck was red too, she told me, because he had

heard. But he would not say anything else and she had remained where she was.

Then, becoming serious again, she explained to me the real aim of Caritas. "We want to found a secular institute," she said. Since I did not understand what that was, she went on to quote from the Holy Father on the matter of secular institutes. The group was to remain a lay group, but the members were to make at least the vow of chastity and be resolved to follow this work for life. She showed me the beautiful wedding ring she had designed for herself and Mary Linda. She had already made her vow and Mary Linda intended to make it soon. They planned a simple ceremony around it. Kathleen did not know yet what she wanted to do, nor did Marcella, so they had no rings.

Bertha asked me what I thought about vows for lay groups. I said, "I will leave that to the future staff workers of the house. I will welcome and long for some to come who want to give themselves to God by vow, for I believe, personally, that a vow is the best safeguard and stabilizer. Yet I will also welcome those who want to give themselves for a short time only. God does not call us all in the same way. And the lay life is not the religious life. What is necessary in a convent may be superfluous in a community of lay people, or a source of pride, or otherwise a stumbling-block. There is a part for those who take vows and for those who do not. Some from the house may well meet others with whom they will want to marry. They will start new Catholic families with a greater understanding and appreciation of the Sacrament of Matrimony than those who have never had the experience of giving, of poverty, of sacrifice and suffering which is a part of our life at the house, no matter how long one stays."

I agreed with her that some member or members of lay groups ought to be wholly given to God, if not by vow, at least by resolution, for the stability of the group. "But it is all a question of love," I went on. "Out of love, one seeks God's glory and not one's own. And in love, God draws us to Himself in His own way, in the measure and degree that pleases Him."

We talked about a lot of things then. Dr. McGrauer is a sociologist and a teacher, and we exchanged ideas on children and education and environment and social work.

That night I talked to a mixed group at Caritas about the house and work in Memphis. They all seemed greatly interested, and gave me money to help the work at the house.

Butch and I spent a few days there in New Orleans and went swimming in the lake and riding in the car with our friends at Caritas. We offered with them their weekly dialogue Mass on Saturday. I spoke for a little while to the group who met for Mass preparation in their parish church, and to Dr. McGrauer's class at Xavier. Everyone seemed interested in the house, and I was cheered by their interest in us and in other lay movements in the Church.

At last the time came to say goodbye, but once more I promised to return next year if possible to the day camp to learn something about crafts. I had another reason for promising, too. I had visited the Shrine of St. Roch and promised a visit of thanksgiving if he would obtain a cure for Butch's leg, which was still in a long leg brace.

When I left I promised to tell anyone I met who was interested in the lay apostolate, but who did not want to work with me in Memphis, about Caritas, and they promised to do the same in reverse. We promised to pray for each other, especially for workers, for never was it more true than now that "the fields are white with the harvest," or more necessary to "pray to the Lord of the harvest that He send laborers into His fields."

At home once more, I found the house and the work about the same, plenty of babies and plenty of children, and people who were poor and whose poverty brought its own problems.

One day one of the mothers (who had two little boys in the nursery) told me that she was very unhappy because, although born a Catholic, she had left the Church some years ago, before the children were born, and not returned. Now she had two children and one on the way, and her husband was drinking and making things very difficult for her. She was afraid of him, she was sick in conscience and wanted to come back to God and the haven of His House. But she lacked the courage, and asked my prayers. Gladly I promised them, wishing there was more I could do.

"Wouldn't your husband consent to being married in the Church?" I asked her.

She was sure he would not. And by now she was not sure she wanted him to. She was afraid of the permanence of a sacramental marriage. Awakening in her was a love of God, and with it a fear of going further against His will. If she returned to the Church and had her marriage blessed by a priest, she would feel obliged to stick to it somehow, she said. And in these years she had grown to know her husband well enough to wonder if that were best, or even possible. She was so mixed up, she said, she did not know what to do.

Until this time I had considered the house too small to give shelter to others, but faced with this new problem I offered hospitality if it should ever be needed. And she promised to come to me if things became unendurable.

147

A few weeks later Butch and I were coming home from a visit with Mother and I was dressing him for bed when the telephone rang.

"This is Denise Mitchell," the voice said. "I've decided to come back into the Church. And Mitchell has told us we can get out then. Can we come?"

"Come on," I invited. And that is how Denise became a friend and a part of the house. That is also the beginning of a new phase in the existence of the house, for it was then that I learned that you can give much, having little, if you love much. And Blessed Martin House became a house of hospitality indeed, offering shelter as well as those other things, to Christ in His least brethren.

15

After Denise came, she began helping me one day a week, her day off. She was still working, and hoped to continue for as long as possible in order to have money for the baby when it was born and for her family afterward, when she would leave the house and set up housekeeping for herself again.

The other mothers of children in the nursery were also, for the most part, conscientious in helping with the work, although there are always a few who do as little as possible, and that reluctantly. Nevertheless, the important work was done because somehow there was always someone to pitch in when the going was roughest. Anne was good at that and Elnora, and of course there was always my mother, and Ida, the woman who lived across the street and was always so helpful.

There were two or three other volunteers too. I had talked at one of the Catholic schools at a meeting of the C.S.M.C. (Catholic Students' Mission Crusade), and some of the high school girls were thus interested in the house. There were two from Holy Names and some from Sacred

Heart, and some college girls from Sienna who came once a month to help for a few hours. There were Mary Jo and Verna and several others who came. Then there was a young doctor's wife, mother of two children, who came for an hour most weeks and who for a long time paid our laundry bill, until it became too much for her. That was Jean, and all the children loved her. She told them stories and played with them and always brought some nice surprise for them to eat.

Occasionally there were others, too. Hattie Wake came often to bring things to the children, and she would play with them, but she would not change diapers, and I had the feeling she was a little afraid of my brown babies. There was one colored volunteer too, besides Ida, a wonderful woman, Mrs. Becton, who, though never a mother herself, had already raised twenty-seven children. I could call her any time an emergency arose or something special came up, and ask her to take over the house for me, and usually she would do it. She was so capable and full of love for the children and understanding of their needs and problems, together with the peculiar problem of the house itself, that I always felt at peace when she was in charge, as I did not always with some of the others. She understood well why the house existed and was not impatient or disillusioned by its poverty or failures, or frightened at the amount of work it involved.

Then there was Bob. I have to say something special about him because, like Mrs. Becton and Ida, he was in a class by himself. He was young and white, a college student. He was a part of the Outer Circle study group and took part in all the discussions, leading some of them. Like Mrs. Becton, too, he understood the deeper spiritual realities behind the house and saw more than the simple acts of charity that went into caring for babies, or sheltering the homeless, or feeding the hungry. He understood why I could say, "I loved God in these." Yet he saw how necessary these acts of mercy were too, and he came down at least once a week to help at the house. Usually he was the one who came while I went to the doctor for pneumothorax treatments every week or two, and while I was gone, he really took care of the house, alone or with Ida's help. He answered the telephone, answered letters, fixed broken beds or tables and chairs, and on many an occasion diapered and dressed the babies. Only a man could fix a diaper like some I saw on the babies he changed, but fancy or not, it served the purpose for which diapers are used.

All the children loved him, but none as much as Butch did. Butch always ran to him when he came, to be petted and tossed into the air and teased gently, and Bob always obliged.

One day Butch embarrassed both of us and set Bob's face flaming by insisting that Bob was his father. "Bob is my daddy," he said.

That didn't change anything, though, and Bob kept coming and helping, and playing with Butch and the other children as much as ever. He tried to organize a ball team for the boys, but before they were really organized school started and he had to leave.

However, that is getting ahead of my story again. Until that time, he was always there when we needed him, staying late after the children had gone every night, talking with me of God and poverty and the love of these things in a way that stayed with me and comforted me in many a black moment when discouragement crept at me from all sides. If he could be convinced of the good of this way of life which embraced such complete poverty and abandonment to God's will and love for Him in the poorest, the meanest, and the most unlovable, so could others. I would keep trying. So through him Our Lord was pleased to give me hope and encouragement, and pleased to banish much of the suffering of being alone for a time.

Besides these volunteers, there were several people with cars who volunteered to carry the children to a park or out in the country, to fish or play, once a week.

Almost every day we were able to go somewhere. That was necessary after the hot weather set in because it was unbearable indoors, yet there was no place for the children to play outdoors. We had no yard and were on a busy street. Sometimes I let the larger children play on the sidewalk, but they would forget and run into the street to retrieve a ball or a toy and there was always the danger there of one of them being hit by a car. I was afraid for them, and so I asked the pastor of the white parish church we attended to let us use his yard and he gladly consented. On the days when we did not go to a park, or on some other outing, the children played there.

Nevertheless the park was better, because in it there were swings, a wading pool, slides and a sand pile, plus the feeling the children had of "going out." In Father's yard there was only the grass, and the few toys we brought from the house. Sometimes the children would leave it of their own accord to come back to Blessed Martin House, which meant crossing one street.

Members of the Outer Circle would carry us to the park, zoo, or country, leave us, and return for us at an appointed time. Albert Morris, Eugenia, Gattas, Carol James, John Fletcher, Clark Porteous, Phyllis O'Callaghan,

Father Wiley, Father Coyne, and occasionally others would do this.

Morris was especially considerate. Though neither he nor his wife was a Catholic, all their children were, and both husband and wife loved the Church and were always willing to help the house. Morris would take us out in his truck, often twice a week. Besides that, he did most of the hauling we needed. If someone gave us a couch or a bed or clothing, it was Morris we called to pick it up for us. If we had a surplus of clothing and wanted to take some down to Holly Springs to the Catholic school there where many children were in need, it was on Morris we called. He worked nights and was supposed to sleep days, but how often he cheerfully gave up a day's rest for us! He had six children of his own, and he knew what children needed. He was colored himself and knew how difficult colored women find it to make a living for themselves and their families. He was not surprised or shocked to find how many resorted to sin, to illicit love affairs, to make ends meet. On the contrary, he often argued that it was necessary, and hardly would believe that some women alone in those circumstances did not, that by God's grace such virtue is possible. He admitted few exceptions, and these only of individuals he knew personally. I could not convince him, but neither could I agree with him. I understood him. In fact, every day at the house, I could see more and more reasons for his doubts and disillusionment.

Outside of the professional class: nurses, teachers, social workers, etc., there is practically nothing a Negro woman here can do and get paid a living wage. The department stores, hotels, hospitals, factories, and housewives who hire domestic help, all pay about the same thing—fifteen to eighteen dollars a week, with sometimes, but not always, carfare. On the same job, doing the same work, white employees get more, there are no unions to make the pay equal. On union jobs, most often no Negroes are hired at all. So the Negro woman, wherever she works, remains a maid, a servant, with the salary of a servant, and does the lowest, dirtiest, most unwanted job in the place. She can't better her condition by changing jobs because the other jobs are the same. She can educate herself for some profession only if she has the time, money, and mental capacity. Her educational background, her chance for schooling in the lower grades, has probably ill prepared her for any professional training. If she already has family responsibilities, she has not the time, nor the money either.

In season, she can pick cotton, if she knows how, and the pay is good. But the hours are long (from four-thirty or five in the morning, often until dark, or about five or six o'clock). The work is hard. And if she has children, she has hardly any time for them at all.

Some of the mothers at Blessed Martin House picked cotton. They brought their children to us at about five in the morning and picked them up about seven or eight at night. They were tired by then, and the children too, and the latter sleepy as well. That made good parent-child relationships difficult.

Besides this, there was the influence of their environment, the heritage of many generations of oppression, and socially encouraged low moral standards—encouraged by tolerant attitudes of white authorities, white ministers, white law enforcement officers, and the white society in which we must live. Other people speak of the "double standard," but down here there has always been a triple standard: what is morally acceptable for women, what is morally acceptable for men—and what is morally acceptable for Negroes. By this last standard, almost anything goes—or used to go—as long as it did not involve white people. Only in rather recent times has the Negro been accounted morally responsible for his own actions here. Even yet there are many who do not consider him so—people in places where they ought not be (on police forces, in courtrooms as judges, on newspapers as editors).

So there is a strong background of public opinion among the poorest and most ignorant Negroes, in city slums, and even in better Negro neighborhoods in cities, which condones sexual immorality as "natural" and accepts common law "marriages" and their impermanence with placid indifference, and divorce and remarriage are regarded as steps *up* in the moral scale because intelligence has conformed to civil law in directing the law of the senses.

Often I have heard "respectable" colored matrons, even social "leaders," tell others, or had them tell me, that "once you've had a man, you have to keep on with it, or you'll go crazy. It's a natural thing. God created Eve for Adam. He didn't mean for a woman (or a man) to live alone."

There is no concept of a consecrated virginity, a fruitful virginity, but virginity is seen as a sterile thing, empty and cold. Love and lust have somehow become confounded until they are considered identical. And it is lust, paraded under the name of love, that is shown at movie theatres, on the stage, even at amateur nights for children and young people, in "art" and books about Negroes, novels and short stories. And lust breathes under the lush music from the jukeboxes in cafés and railroad stations, and the records from the big record stores on Beale Street. And lust leers from the billboard advertise-ents and mocks in the tolerant laughter of those who "have nothing against Negroes as long as they stay in their place."

And all around there is no other love, and often, it seems, no pleasure nor consolation but those of the body. Spirit and dignity are crushed under the weight of hatred, intolerance and discrimination; stifled in back seats, movie lofts, back-door service and back-street amusement places. God's own Church left them for years in the hands of a few missionaries, often men with neither love nor understanding for Negroes, but only with a great missionary zeal to help them through great trials by some hit-or-miss method. The parish churches often pretended they didn't exist, or acted as if, in their existence, they were millions of miles away.

"Help the poor Negro Mission." Not poor because it's away in Africa, but poor because, though across the street, it is an almost infinite distance from the heart or mind of this people, this congregation. The other Churches gave even less than this, and often taught that the Negro is an inferior race, accursed of God for the sin of Ham, deserving of the scorn and contempt of other more blessed races. All manner of injustice, barbarity, and inhumanity was excused—nay, more, *sanctified*—by the distorted words of Him who was the Truth and Love and who died for all men.

So the Negro made his own churches and faiths, following the Bible as he understood it, and the pattern of the white churches around him, churches where Christ was being crucified anew in His members and rent asunder.

The colored man was crushed, too, in mind by rundown or ramshackle schools, poor teachers, split sessions (to allow students to go to the fields to pick cotton), with classes held in the hottest days of summer, when the mind is dullest. Crushed in body by inadequate medical care, poor diets, lack of love and security and clothing.

When a girl grows up thus, surrounded by this, who is to wonder at her suffering, or mock her shame or sneer at her sin? "Let him who is without sin among you cast the first stone," Our Lord said to the doctors of the law, the leaders, the holiest ones of Israel. What would He have said to us, who by our own sinful actions and examples and sinful omissions have been responsible in part for the sins of others?

This I knew was what Morris saw, but I knew also that he could not see beyond it the grace of God that somehow kept some pure, some unspotted for Himself. He could not see the struggle of some who kept their integrity through suffering and sneers. He said, "You don't know women like I do."

That was no time for confession, and Morris was not a priest, so I did not feel that it was necessary for me to explain that I knew the temptations of a woman and that if God preserved me from some sins, it was for His greater glory, and if He had allowed me to fall headlong into others, it was for my humility. Nor did I think it necessary to say which was which. I said instead, "I know more about those things than you think I know. I don't believe anyone can love God very much unless he could also love some person very much. And the greatest sinner would possibly have made the greatest saint. That is the worst thing about sin—the prostitution of a soul. Mary Magdalene was a great sinner and a great saint because 'she loved much.' If these women you are talking about could be convinced that God is real, and His love is real and can accept a real love in return, do you know they would be, I'll bet, much closer to Christ than a lot of women I know who think themselves so holy because they are 'respectable,' who wear a ring on their finger and have ice in their hearts, and syrup on their lips that sickens you."

Morris had something nasty to say then about "respectable women" who made a show of piety and religion. It wasn't very nice, but I didn't chide him at this time, because I felt a secret agreement with his sentiments.

Besides helping us in so many other ways he also brought us food from time to time. He liked to hunt and fish and always brought us some of what he caught. Often when we went fishing, he stayed with us, and once I remember we waded into a bar pit and caught a lot of fish in an old curtain, all the while looking up the hill for a game warden, but none came. We caught all kinds of fish that day, big and little, and went home proudly swinging our strings, sorry we couldn't brag about how we got them.

He was also good at fixing things around the house, together with Bob and Dan Hanrahan, and when something went wrong we were quick to get on the telephone and call "Morris!"

Rosemary, his wife, was helpful in other ways. With six children of her own to care for, she was like most of the special friends of the house—Porteous, Hanrahan, Gattas, etc. She helped by sewing, writing, or interesting others in the house. Her home too, like those of other special friends, was a haven when I was tired and needed peace and quiet. I could go there and read or sleep or simply relax, or talk things out, finding help and relief by bringing my problems up for airing. And often I practiced my arguments on her and Morris, they taking the other side even when really they agreed with me.

There is one more volunteer I have to mention especially, Linda John. That is not her real name, but it will do. She was a convert as I was, white, Southern, and from a family which had no great love either for Catholics or Negroes. She became interested in the house, I think, out of her love for Blessed Martin really, although she had been a member of the study group before.

At least once a week she would take us some place in her car, and each time on our way we would talk about things more important than the place we were going; about race and wages, about Communism and Capitalism, about the Catholic Worker and Dorothy Day. We would talk about the mothers and the work at Blessed Martin House, and sometimes our words became very warm indeed. Yet over the months our friendship grew strong enough to take all the sting out of our disagreements, probably because we really wanted the same thing, God's will, and His love manifest in our lives and those of others.

Sometimes she would come to the house to get the laundry, and wash it in her machine, after our other friend had stopped sending out things to the laundry for us. While the clothing washed in the machine we would visit and talk. When we were poorest she would give us money or food, although actually she did not have a great deal herself—she had a large family and a moderate income. But she was willing to share what she had.

That impressed me most, because she really did not agree with me. She did not think the nursery should be free. She did not agree that Negro maids should be paid more, either, nor even that the Negro as a whole was ready in any other sense for real equality. She regarded me as an exception and sometimes was openly (to me, since I understood her) resentful when other colored friends of mine or people at the house addressed her by her first name or acted in at all a familiar manner.

One day we got into one of our arguments about wages. First begging me to take no offense personally (and I did not—she was one whose sincerity I never doubted, even in those later days when I would suffer great torment from doubt of some of my friends because their skin was paler than my own) she said, "You don't know these girls like I do Helen. You say we should pay more, but they aren't worth it. They don't do the work. Most of them don't know how to clean a house—they're careless and undependable. Most of them are lazy and try to get by on sympathy or deceit."

"Then why do you keep them?" I asked. "If you let them go on working for you, day after day, they must do the work well enough to satisfy you, or you wouldn't keep them."

But she denied this vigorously. "No. But we can't find any better. You can count them, the really good maids. Look at Alma" (a woman I had sent to work for a friend of hers). "Now, I know Celeste is easy to work for. She's as nice as she can be. Alma came to work late, or some days she wouldn't come at all. She wouldn't call to say she wasn't coming and Celeste would be waiting for her. If Bobby cried, and Alma was ironing or busy in the kitchen, she'd never stop to see what was wrong with him, to dry him or play with him. If Celeste didn't go to him, she never would. She did her work well, I'll admit that. But she wasn't dependable. And she had no love for the child.

"Then there's a girl I've had myself, off and on for a couple of years or so, Rose. She never cleans the stoves, or dusts the corners and under things. But she has a family and I feel sorry for her, so I let her keep coming. There are a lot of us like that. It's not that we are satisfied with the work, but we know they are almost all like that. We accept that and are patient with it. Sometimes we feel sorry for the girl, because she is trying hard, and keep her, even when we know the work is half done."

"Well then, do you really think that is fair to yourself or the maid, to keep her if she does not do satisfactory work?" I wanted to know. "If you keep her, she thinks you are satisfied, so she never tries to do any better. If you demanded good workers as they do on other jobs and paid a living wage, you could get good workers.

"Did you ever stop to think that the reason many won't do better work is that they have no incentive? Why should they cook your meals and clean your house and mind your babies while neglecting their own?—because they almost have to do that, you know, neglect their own, I mean. When they are working, like some of the mothers here, nine and ten hours a day, for a salary they can't live on, who do you think cares for their homes and children? Some of these women get twelve or fifteen dollars a week. How much would *you* do for twelve or fifteen dollars a week? I know I wouldn't do much for it."

She looked a little skeptical, glancing at the house I kept for nothing, no salary.

"It reminds me of a story I heard about a nun," I continued. "I'm like that nun. I will work all day for nothing—rather, for the love of God. But if I did work for a salary, I'd demand a fair salary and reasonable hours.

"This nun was kneeling washing the ulcers of a woman with leprosy, and a visitor shuddered and drew herself up and back from her, saying 'Oh, I wouldn't do that for a million dollars!' The nun kept on with her work and answered 'Neither would I.' That is exactly how I feel about the work these maids do and the work I do here. They go to work and lose their identity and their dignity. They become 'girls' instead of women and lose their last names altogether. They work as long and as hard as anyone employed in any other job a woman can do, yet they receive the least. A man says he loves his home and family and children more than anything in the world. And he pays the secretary in his office a good salary and the foreman at his factory gets a nice fat check, but the woman who cleans his house, and cooks his food and diapers his babies and looks after his children gets a pittance too small to support herself or her family, and even that she gets grudgingly, or paternally, almost as if it were charity, not salary, all because his wife 'feels sorry' for her. Is that right?"

"No," Linda agreed. "It's not right, exactly. But other people don't see it the way you do. And we can't do anything about it by stirring up hard feeling between the black and the white or between those who have and those who have not."

I agreed with that. "But we can't make that an excuse for continuing injustice, either. The Holy Father says that workmen should receive a just wage. Catholics then, at least, should set an example by paying their maids what is fair. I think from the encyclicals that the Pope teaches unmistakably that if a day's work is done, a just day's wage must be paid, a living wage. If you hire a person who does not satisfy you with his work, you can fire him. But if you keep him, you have to pay him a just salary or be guilty before God of taking from him what is his due."

"All that sounds good, but you just don't understand, Helen. People are not going to pay better salaries unless the work is done better. Maybe, if someone opened a house like this as a training center, where girls could come and really learn to do the work, they could get good salaries. I know some who get good salaries, but they do good work."

"If such a training center did open, what guarantee would these women have of a better salary? Do you think they'd take the training, give the time and effort, on the hope it *might* make wages better? We're going around in circles. It goes back to this: if you pay better wages, more people able to do better work will apply. It's happened in the North. It can happen here. But you can't give the excuse that the work isn't good enough, if you keep the worker, by saying you keep him out of charity. Pope Pius XI, in his encyclical on Atheistic Communism, brings that out. He says that the 'charity' which deprives the working-man (and I'm sure he includes working women as well, especially since he earlier deplores the fact that mothers of families must work outside their own homes at all) of the salary to which he has a strict title in justice is not charity at all, but only its 'empty name and hollow semblance.' He says, 'The wage earner is not to receive as alms what is his due in justice.'"

Linda tried another tactic, as almost invariably happened at this point in our arguments, with something like shame in her tone:

"Another thing you aren't considering is that many families simply can't afford to pay any more. Take me, for instance. I have a large family. I'm not physically able to do all my housework myself, especially the heavy work, but I can't afford to pay more than three dollars and carfare. I just don't have it. I can just make ends meet now, with the little Theresa's help, because of my family. There are many people like me. They pay as much as they can. They can't afford to pay more."

This time it was my turn to apologize first and beg that no personal offense be taken. I said to her what Father Coyne kept saying so many times to people who gave him that same excuse: "Those people don't need a maid, then. I mean, if you can't afford something, you have to do without it. I can't go downtown and say 'I need this coat, but I can't afford to pay the full amount for it,' pay what I have, and walk out with it. It's the same thing."

"All right, then. Suppose all the white people in Memphis who have maids felt like you do, and tomorrow they all let their maids go, because they couldn't afford to pay more than that, or because they wouldn't. Where would all those girls go then? Would they be any better off then not working?"

"I don't know. Not at first, certainly. But if such an unlikely thing did happen, I don't doubt that in a short time the maids would prepare themselves better for that work, or for some other. And it might do a lot of white women some good to have to do their own work themselves. They might well find, after a few days of it, that they can afford to pay more than they thought. At least that would teach them how much work they could justly expect in one day from one woman. But those who can't afford more aren't the only ones paying salaries like this. It is everybody. Maybe some housewives can't afford more, and if they explain that and the maid agrees to work anyway, and the white woman gives her food and clothes, and lots of little helps like that, which add up to a higher salary (as I know many do), it might be different, possibly. But what about the hotels, the hospitals, the cafés, the train stations, the bus stations, and all those other places like that, that are paying Negro women the same as your little families, fifteen or at most twenty dollars a week? Can't they afford anything better either? Is it really the quality of the work? Of course not. It is the race. We can't get around that."

She had to admit they could pay more, but then she offered the usual excuse of racial misunderstanding and intolerance. "You can't change all that in a day," she said.

I pointed out that a considerable number of days had passed since Negro slavery had ended and Negroes had begun to demand recognition as men and women, a demand which, if not met by Christians, might well be met in a way disastrous for both our race and hers, because those who were selfish and atheistic might well meet it for selfish ends, which would destroy all freedom.

"The best thing we can do about it is to pray," she said, "to offer our little trials and crosses, like the Little Flower did."

"That is a good way for religious," I agreed, "but lay people, I believe, must not only pray, but do more also. If we believe in Christ, we have to live the Christ-life, and publicly admit our belief in what He taught in word *and* example. We can't act as if the world is all rosy, because it isn't, or as if we have no part in changing things, because we do."

"I guess I'm just not the active type like you and Dorothy Day. I'd rather do the little things I can, my duties to my family, my novenas, daily Mass when I can, things like that. I don't have the brain for all this other stuff. It's too deep for me."

"Oh, you've got the brain all right. And you keep seeing more and more. I'm impatient and taking out some of what I'd like to say to others on you. But the very fact that you listen and stay my friend shows you are bigger than you think you are. And Our Lord is going to surprise you one day by the great things He will ask of you and you'll do them."

Linda laughed. "Well, you pray for me," she asked. "Maybe your friend Blessed Martin will help me understand, if you ask him. He never does anything for me when I ask him."

"That may be because you ask him for the wrong things, for things you shouldn't have."

"That may be. Then ask him to make me know what things I ought to have."

"I'll do that," I promised.

16

Every day was full at blessed martin house, and every day was different. Some days there were twenty-five children in the nursery, and lunch hour was bedlam. There were infants and pre-school children, and most often only Ida and I to make the soup or occasionally some other dish, and feed them.

The children were wonderful and patient, as the children of the poor learn to be. But all the little babies wanted to eat at the same time. Some of the larger children often helped to feed the little babies, and were very proud of themselves when I permitted it.

Sometimes well-dressed matrons would come in, representing some club or social agency, and find me with a baby on my lap and another in a chair, feeding them both while Ida fixed lunch for the larger children. Packages of clothing we had received for the children or other people who needed them would be sitting on the floor or couch where the mailman or expressman had left them, and we had not yet had time even to glance at them. Here would be a toy some child had forgotten to put up, and there a wet puddle to show all the babies did not have rubber pants. In the back the telephone might be ringing with shrill insistence, and patiently sitting on one of the chairs might be a man or woman, poorly dressed, often dirty, waiting to see me about food or clothing or taking a child.

Sometimes the pretty lady would look around and barely repress a sniff of disdain. Sometimes she would become too effusive, telling me how much she admired me, or Blessed Martin or the house or colored people in general. Often she would tell me I needed more help—but she never offered to give me any. Most who came in this way were of this latter type. They usually said something like this: "You are doing a wonderful work for God. Why don't you get some of the good colored ladies from St. Augustine's or St. Anthony's" (the colored parishes) "to help you?"

I tried to point out that I had tried many times and within the limits set by circumstances of opposition I could not control, was still trying to get some of the "good ladies from St. Augustine's or St. Anthony's" to come down and help me. I tried *not* to say that many of the "good ladies at St. Augustine and St. Anthony's" were like many of the good ladies of St. Anne's and St. Michael's and Blessed Sacrament, and all the other churches, having their own interests and problems and limitations; often they found my way of life as puzzling as she did, and were perhaps even more shamed, scandalized, or antagonized by the poverty of it.

"Why don't you get some of the high school girls at St. Augustine's or St. Anthony's, then? Surely this is what they are learning in school, to help the poor, and these poor colored babies certainly do need you."

I told them "Thanks for the suggestion. I have been

trying to interest the students in the Catholic schools in the work and we do have some volunteers from the high schools, from Sienna and even from Memphis State. So far we don't have any from St. Augustine's. We have had a few in the past from St. Anthony's, but we hope some day there will be more."

"Don't you think you should stick to your own race? I mean, to get them to help you? You should really interest more of your own people, don't you think, bring them into the work?"

"Oh, my God!" I often thought to myself, "what do they think I'm trying to do? Do they think I don't *want* people of my own color, my own race, my own blood? Do they think I *like* being in the middle of both races?"

Was it pride or was it humility that kept me from telling how often, and with what pain and with what love, I have prayed for my own, for those like me whose skins are dark, and whose spirits like mine are crippled, naked, and empty—Simons of Cyrene, crushed under the weight of a cross we do not understand, jerking impatiently, even as he, under it, because we, like him, cannot see whose cross it is we are carrying, except He show us? Yet there is only one Cross, Christ's. All other crucifixions are merely a participation in the One Crucifixion; all other crosses, splinters of the one Cross on which the Son of God died.

Was it pride or was it humility that kept me from revealing what I have offered of myself for this one thing— as if I could bargain with God, as if I could give Him something that was not already His own?

I do not know. I only know I did not say these things. I could not say them. I said, "I wish I could reach more of my own people. But that is not the most important thing.

The most important thing is that people who love God will love each other also and try to help each other, not only friends and people next door, but people in the slums, the destitute and unwanted, who have nothing, physically, mentally, morally, but are wholly poor, and the children of the poor, who are not responsible for their own existence, nor for the ignorances and sins of their parents. So although I would like to have people of my own race come, I am glad if others come instead. In time they *will* come. Meanwhile I encouraged all who believe as I do to come and help at the house, no matter what race they belong to. I think that is the spirit of the Church, One, Holy, and *Catholic*, Universal, for all men. I'm glad the students come from Sacred Heart and Holy Names and Sienna, because they give us both—white and colored—a chance to put into practice the things we say we believe about the Mystical Body of Christ."

Sometimes it seemed to me the other person agreed, but most often in these people I seemed to sense a sort of resentment, a silent, guarded, and perhaps even unwilling antagonism to what I was saying. But it was never expressed in words—not to me, anyway.

One day when Father Coyne was there, a drunken woman across the street lay down on the sidewalk to sleep. Father Coyne had been pastor of a colored church long enough to know the gentle, careful treatment our police give Negro women offenders, especially drunk ones, so he, like me, did not want them to find her there. We went across the street and helped her into the house, and she sat on a couch, looking a little dazed for a while. But after Father left, she would not stay any longer but staggered down the street to her house.

We had given her nothing; we helped her in no real

way, because another day, away from us, she fell into the same thing and the consequences of it. The pretty ladies would not have understood that, and in the eyes of some men it may seem foolish, futile, a waste of love.

But that wasted, foolish, futile action did more to establish Father Coyne in the heart of the people of that neighborhood than anything else he did, even those unquestionably worthy acts of charity for the children which had become his habit; taking them to the park, showing movies, begging up things for a party for them. It convinced them of the genuineness and depth of his love and care for them, for us. It took away the last doubts, suspicions, and distrust of the "white man" by showing them the priest, the true father who loves also the prodigal sons, surfeiting themselves on the husks of swine.

Was it wasted? Was it foolish? Was it futile?

How many other of our actions done for pure love of God may appear in the eyes of human reason, human prudence, human understanding so foolish, so wasted, so fruitless, yet have even more far-reaching effects in the hidden depths of other human souls? "We are fools for Christ," St. Paul says, "but you are wise. . . . Men revile us and we answer with a blessing. . . . Follow my example then, I entreat you, as I follow Christ's." It is a hard saying. But Peter Maurin says the hard saying is the reason the book is written.

As I have said, in the evenings when they got off from work, the mothers would help with the work at the house. Usually each mother came one evening. She was tired, often hot and depressed after a full day's work, and it was not easy for her to come to more work at Blessed Martin House and then go home to more work still. We tried—I and whoever else worked with me—to get most of the work done in the day, to make it easier, but still there was always plenty to be done. Some mothers persevered in bringing children because the children were loved and cared for and kept dry and clean. Often they would come home to find children completely dressed up and spotless in "new" clothing which had come in that day and been distributed among those who needed it. This meant a lot to those who were poorest, and often did wonders toward reviving depressed spirits and extreme weariness and discouragement. Still the turnover in children was rapid, because some mothers could or would not bring themselves to fall into the spirit of cooperation necessary to keep the nursery open at the house.

"I'm tired," was a frequent excuse I heard as I watched a mother dress her child to take it home, leaving me alone to clean up or to clean over the things she was supposed to have cleaned. Or, "I'm sick. I'll help Friday." "I really can't help tonight. I've got to go to the doctor." "I've got to go to see my aunt, she's sick."

The mothers' meetings held once a month to discuss the problems of the House, particularly of the nursery, helped some. Cooperation was better then, as the mothers learned to know me better, and each other. Occasionally too we had parties for the mothers, and that helped the spirit of belonging.

"This is your nursery," I kept reminding them. "We all have a part in keeping it, or it won't be. Because our parts are different, doesn't mean all parts aren't important. I see that the rent is paid, and the gas and lights and other bills, not by myself, but with money that comes into the house for that purpose. When you aren't here, I take care of the babies and clean and do whatever has to be done. When you are here, then you too should be willing to clean or care for the babies, or do whatever has to be done. And you should all care for the other babies as carefully as you want me or the other mothers to care for yours."

At mothers' meeting, the mothers said they saw this. "We ought to be willing to take care of the other mothers' children. Someone is taking care of ours," one might say.

"I don't know what I would do without the house," another might add. "I'm willing to do all I can to help."

"Yes, I think all the mothers ought to pitch in and help," someone else would say. On and on around the mulberry bush. It sounded good, but how quickly the good resolutions of many seemed to melt under the harsh light of reality when it was their day to help with the house.

After Denise came to live at the house, it became even more difficult to get some mothers to cooperate. Many were envious or resented Denise's presence, partly through her own fault, perhaps unconscious fault, of almost invariably saying the wrong thing at the wrong time or in a wrong way that antagonized. Partly it was because some felt that because she lived there, she should do more.

I did not feel so. The nursery, I tried to explain, was to be regarded as a sort of cooperative, all receiving according to their needs, all giving according to their ability. I made this distinction because most mothers who have children in the nursery are working, although for very small salaries. They are, in a sense, independent because of that, because if they want to make a greater sacrifice than working at the house, and want to do without other things they need or want very much for their good or the good of their children, they can take their children elsewhere. So they are at the nursery by their own choice.

But people who come to the house for shelter are different; they have a real, immediate, and fundamental need. They come, not so much through their own choice, as through harsh circumstances that force on them the real charity of some person or the impersonal "charity" of the taxpayers through social welfare agencies. They are Christ, who says again, "The birds have nests and the foxes have holes, but the Son of man has no place to lay His head." They come then as guests, if their need is great, and not as fellow workers, except by their own choice. The exception is made when they continue to remain at the house after their immediate need is satisfied and they have returned to work or to the ability to work at a living wage.

These become, if they will it, members of our "family," and are no longer guests after this time. If they choose to remain then, they do have work to do as in a family, and other rules to follow, which do not apply to the mothers who come to the nursery, or others temporarily receiving shelter.

Some mothers seemed to understand this when I tried to explain it to them, others did not. Most, I think, did not. But I believe that this was due largely to Denise's attitude at that time, which had to grow and broaden, as we all do in our attitudes. She had closed herself up tight in a shell lest someone should love her and have to be loved in return, and she was afraid of love. Only Love Himself could break through the hard crust of that shell to bring her out to light and love through His own love. And He did, opening her to our love, too. But that was yet a long time off. The mothers could not see it and did not understand it. Neither did some members of the Outer Circle and friends of the house, and friends of my own. Some would not come any more, convinced that this was the final proof of my madness, or my pride —for many say I am proud. I do not know. God knows. May He bring me finally to humility, if I am, for I have nothing of which to be proud but a multitude of sins that only an infinity of mercy could pardon.

But they would not come any more and I could not explain or they would not understand when I did. God, in His love, has His own ways of breaking attachments which we have not the courage to break, of breaking the cords that keep us in some measure from Himself. "It is an awful thing to fall into the hands of the living God." But when you have thrown yourself into those hands, you know it is the greatest thing that ever happened to you, or could happen to you. You want to be detached and humble, and you glory in your dependence on God. Poverty is a treasure of great price and suffering becomes joy—not either thing of itself but because these are things God has chosen.

After Denise came I was able to go out more to visit Mother, or call on Mr. Childs to read the C.U.S.A. letter to him and answer it, because Denise would stay with the children. Then in the summer when Friendship House invited me to go up and give a course at the summer school at Burnley, Virginia (for Washington Friendship House) and spend a week there for vacation, I felt I could accept, although I had never been away from the house for so long a period. The Catholic Worker retreat was scheduled around that time too, and the fare from Friendship House would be enough to cover that fare too if I went on the bus instead of the train. That would mean a whole month away from the house, but I certainly needed the retreat, Father Coyne and I decided, and the other things were almost as important. So I should go, we decided, if I could depend on Denise to be at the house at night and Mother and Ida to care for the house in the daytime.

I talked it over with all of them, and the arrangement was satisfactory to all. Denise was going to daily Mass and Communion by now, and I felt certain that I could depend on her to keep her word. Besides that, there were her own two youngsters at the nursery and the one on the way, which made it unlikely that she would want to be away from home at night.

My nephew, Lawrence, promised to feed the cat and puppy, and Mrs. Becton promised to come down and help whenever Mother needed her at the house, and of course Father Coyne would be around to see that things went well.

With these reassurances, Butch and I left for New York, for the Catholic Worker retreat, since it came before the summer school at Friendship House by a week and a few days.

17

THE TRIP TO NEW YORK WAS UNEVENTFUL. AS UNOBTRU-
sively as possible I tested the effectiveness of the recent
Supreme Court decisions regarding interstate travel for
Negroes. Butch and I took a seat near the back, but not
all the way back. When the bus began to fill, we did not
move back but gave white passengers the choice of asking
us to move, standing, or sitting behind us. I did this
with only an apparent calm, for inwardly I was terribly
afraid. I think I am a coward at heart. I was scared, but
made up in my mind what I would say if someone asked
me to move. Meanwhile I pretended to be very much
interested in a book I was reading to Butch. From the
corner of my eye, I saw some white people come back,
hesitate, then return to the front. I pretended to be totally deaf to the comments of other members of my own
race in the back who were speaking about me. One was
saying what she thought Negroes *ought* to get, and are
sure to get, who defy Southern traditions.

"Yeah, our people just brings things on themself.
When you know you got to be back, you oughta go
back."

"Umhumn, child, don't I know it? When one of them knock her flat or somethin' then she'll learn."

"Yeah, white folks sure does you dirty, don't they —but we got to live here and we might as well make it easy on our own selves."

"Child, yes. Don't you know it. God don't like mighty. He gonna bring it down and come in His glory."

"Amen."

After a while a white couple, after hesitating, took the seats behind us. The bus driver came back, looked around counting seats, and went back to the door. Some more people got on, some soldiers, colored and white. All of them took seats behind us too.

I was in an agony of suspense until the bus driver actually started the bus, as I remembered a time, only a few years before, after one of the first Supreme Court decisions in this regard. The girl who rented pillows in Nashville had insisted that a friend and I move back. We had refused. She brought the bus driver back, and he insisted we move. We quoted the court's decision and refused again. He went away and returned in a few minutes. When he came back he had a big, burly, red-faced policeman with him. The latter's gun swung loosely on his hip. He played meaningfully with a big club in one hand. "You girls get back in the back where you belong," he ordered us.

Once more we quoted the court decision. With a curse, he lifted his club and told us what he thought of the decision and repeated his order. I was not nearly as ready to be a martyr for the cause of racial justice as I had believed. Neither was my friend. We moved back.

But no one said anything this time, though there were some glares, which I pretended not to see or feel. Of course in the rest stops, the pattern was the same as of old, nothing for colored often but a table in a dirty kitchen (seeing some of the kitchens I learned to envy less those who ate in the big shiny restaurants outside) where I would not eat, and smelly toilets with no place to wash your hands. Butch got sick, as usual, so eating wasn't too much of a problem, since he could not retain much anyway.

The second day on the bus we crossed the Mason-Dixon line and became people again with rights, and I could breathe in peace. I could take the chip off my shoulder. It was beginning to scratch a bit and I was glad to take it down. I was going to Virginia, to Friendship House, to learn, on one hand, and to try in some measure to teach, on the other (those who I was sure knew more about this already than I did), how to love God more in others as well as in Himself. I could not talk about a love I did not embrace, and since Christian love is an act of the will, which we are bound to make, I had to embrace it. I kept reminding myself that God made me what I am, a Negro, to live in this time, and this place, here and now to become a saint. Sometimes, in my humiliation, I felt anger surge up in me, and something very akin to hate peeped over the brink of my consciousness, looking for a way in. I might have opened the doors if God hadn't also given me a sense of humor which suddenly saw the incongruity of my loving God, and daydreaming in church in His Presence of giving myself wholly to Him, even my life for Him, and then complaining at the same time of having to suffer these little things so contrary to my own will and nature.

I could see it then. We are willing to die for our faith —provided we can do it our own way. We want to be martyrs (we think) who are roasted or broiled or be-headed, but the daily martyrdom of suffering and humiliation that is our lot, we cannot endure. We make all sorts of excuses, and they sound good, and in themselves sometimes are good, why we should not endure *this* pain, *this* humiliation, *this* failure. The honor of family, of country, of race, of profession. We say, "I wouldn't mind for myself, but for Butch . . . but as a Negro . . . but as one of the working classes . . ."

It's the everlasting paradox of the Christian life, to be most wise when we are most foolish in the eyes of others, and most alive when we are dead to ourselves.

There really is a time when this reasoning and these excuses are valid, when one can in fact change things and ought not in conscience to endure *this* shame, *this* dishonor, *this* particular humiliation or suffering without a struggle, out of love of God in our neighbor; just as there is a time when one must, out of love of God in Himself. Wisdom consists in knowing which is which, and wisdom is a gift of God. It comes little by little as we grow closer to Him; meanwhile we fumble and stumble around in the dark, blessed really by the blindness that hides from us our mistakes. If we saw, we might lose courage and go back. . . .

> God give me the courage to change things that ought
>   to be changed,
> Patience to accept things which cannot be changed,
> And wisdom to know the difference.

Somewhere I read that, and I've thought a lot about it. I thought about it then, smiling to myself in the darkness of a Greyhound bus speeding over the hills, laughing at my own inconsistency. I thought of something Linda had said one day when we were talking about abandonment. "Thy will be done, but Lord, please let me have my own way."

"Oh yes, Lord, send me a cross, I'll gladly bear it for You. But not just any old cross, a plain old wooden one—that one won't do—see here, I've drawn up a few specifications . . ."

"Mother, what are you laughing about?" Butch wanted to know.

"I was thinking you have a silly little mother."

"No, you ain't," Butch objected. "You're a sweet little mother. Let's play Birds Fly."

We arrived in New York at last. The first day I called a few friends to let them know that Butch and I had arrived safely. I had planned to take him to Staten Island where the Smiths lived, who had promised to keep him while I was on retreat at Newburgh. However, his aunt wanted to keep him, and I consented. Thus the next day found us in Harlem instead of on Staten Island. Aunt Marion, Uncle Johnny, Betty and Diana were all well. Betty had been sick and in the "san" too, but now she was well. I did not see my husband and I was glad of that. I have taught Butch to love the father he doesn't remember seeing, but I have never wanted to have him of divided heart or loyalties. I know that pain, having grown up in a broken home myself. So for all our sakes I have been glad that Butch's father has forgotten us.

After I left Butch, I went back to the Catholic Worker, then up to the retreat house, at Maryfarm in Newburgh.

I went up by boat. It was a quiet and pleasant trip. The smell of salt was in the air, fresh and clean, and the water was calm, except for the foam fairies that danced from the boat's motors. Gulls questioned bits of driftwood, then sailed back high into the cool air to serenade the heavens with their funny cries.

I thought about the house in Memphis, wondered about it. It was so small, so unimportant, like a bit of that white foam that floated for a moment on the waters beneath me, then disappeared forever. Was it really worth it? Did it really do any lasting good? Would it really ever change anything—even me? St. Paul said, "We are fools for Christ." That was all right, that was good. But suppose we are just fools? Was this work really God's idea, or my own? Those were some of the questions I knew I wanted to find answers to on the retreat.

I arrived in Newburgh just in time for dinner. I had time to meet only one or two people before the silence began for the retreat following benediction of the Blessed Sacrament.

Father Paul Judge was the retreat master. After the first conference I knew that the retreat was the same one I had made three years previously in New Kingsington, Pennsylvania, with Father Meenan. Before, it had turned my life upside down and inside out. I had been completely, or almost completely, self-centered and bound up and chained by cares for material things, human values and human standards of good. The retreat had made me God-centered instead, and set glowing in my heart a spark which over the years had blown brighter and brighter, until now it was a flame of love consuming me wonderfully in a desire to lose myself in God's love, and have His standards and values. I wondered what it would do now. I hoped it would help me answer the questions that troubled me. I hoped it would help me to grow in the way God wanted me to grow.

As before, the days of the retreat had about them a sort of other-worldly character. You were a part of a living community that breathed joy as each member worked at some task, or studied or prayed or thought in turn; yet in the silence you were alone, just you and God. The silence did not separate you from the other members of the community, but it joined instead, peacefully and warmly, in such a way that one did not invade the privacy of another's being.

My days there were full. In the morning we all said the office of Prime at six. Then we sang Mass together or all gave the responses in a dialogue Mass. How much we felt at one with the priest as we all visibly offered the Holy Sacrifice together. We were not spectators, but *offerers*, with the priest, of the Mass and its fruits. After Mass there was breakfast and one of the retreatants read from the life of Bl. Margaret Clitheroe (as at all meals). When breakfast was finished we all helped with the work, washing the dishes or cleaning the dormitories or the conference room.

The conferences began at nine and lasted about an hour each. Then there was meditation in the chapel. In the conferences Father Judge reminded us that we are made for God's glory and our happiness lies in fulfilling the purpose for which we are made. He reminded us too of the great dignity that has come to us through Christ in our baptism, so that we have become or can become, more than mere creatures, children, sons, co-heirs with Christ! What an obligation, then, as well as privilege, do we have to think as children, behave as children, and in all things to order our lives as becomes children of such a father! It was a great gift to us when God gave us reason and all those qualities that make us human, but

He has given us even more than this. He has given us grace, a share in His own Divine Life, so that we have become more than merely human—sons of God!

Once more I was struck with a deep sense of awe at the thought of God's love. There is so little love in the world (and in our blacker moments, sometimes it seems so little worth loving) that we can scarcely believe in such a Love, surely not comprehend it. "What is man, that Thou art mindful of him?" the Psalmist asks, and we can understand his wonder. Before the world was made, from all eternity, God saw you and saw me, and loved us as He willed to make us and planned the graces He would give each of us to make it possible for us to share His life, if we but willed it; if we but accepted what He offered us!

Father Judge reminded us that we prove our love by preference. God has surrounded us with people and things that are good and beautiful and lovable which we may choose to draw us closer to Him and His love, or which we may choose as His rivals. Sometimes we use things for His glory, and our need. Sometimes we forego the use of things for that same reason. It's a question of love, of preference, of motive, that makes the difference.

And he reminded us that the Cross, that suffering, failure and humiliations are part of *the joy* of the *Christian life*. They are not things that come in spite of it. They are a part of it. Christ did not triumph in spite of His Passion, the horror of the cross and the failure of death, but because of it. And we who share His life triumph in the same way. We, in His Mystical Body, "fill up those things that are wanting of the sufferings of Christ," as St. Paul says, "for His Body, which is the Church," not as if there were really anything wanting, so that our redemption is not complete, but as members of His Mystical

Body, sharing His life. The folly of the Cross is the wisdom of God, for the foolishness of God is wiser than men, and the weakness of God is stronger than men." The things that seem to us so foolish, so hard or so painful, are part of growing up in the Christian life, as crawling and stumbling and walking are part of growing up in our children's lives. How foolish it might seem to a dog to see a baby struggling so painfully to stand and walk on two legs, when the dog is making such nice progress on four. But how tragic would it seem to the child's mother, and later to the child himself, as he became a man, if he spent his life crawling!

Then there were practical conferences on prayer and the interior life, on contemplation and on the applications of the doctrine considered in the earlier conferences.

There were two morning conferences, followed by lunch, then a two-hour rest period. During this time I took long walks out in the fields. The days were beautiful and warm and still, with the smell of ripening fruit in the air and only the sound of bird songs to break the silence, except for the occasional drone of an airplane overhead. I sat on the rocks sometimes, down at the back of the garden where there were outdoor Stations of the Cross, and read or meditated on the material of the conferences or the books I had been reading.

Mostly I read from the life of the Curé d'Ars, or St. Bernadette. When I was tired I read from *The Mass of Brother Michel*. I tried again to read St. Teresa of Avila because she was mentioned with St. John of the Cross in the conferences. I could read him and understand something of what I read, but she antagonized me, and I could not concentrate. After a day or so, I gave it up and read the other books. I was not ready for St. Teresa's writings.

I prayed to her especially though, and to Our Lady,

and Blessed Martin, whom I had loved so lately. I especially wanted him to help me find the answers to my questions and help me fight prejudice in myself, against races, my own and others, and against the really poor. I did not have with me a copy of his life to read, although Father Georges had sent me several copies from Blessed Martin Guild when he sent the statue for our house. Nevertheless I thought a lot of his life, and how like many of his problems must have been to my own. Yet in Christ, and for Him, he had conquered. I wanted his secret, and he showed it to me. It was love. It was a love bigger than all the evils of the world, a capacity for love so big that only God could fill it, and where God had filled it, there was no room for anything else but love.

After the rest period there were two more conferences, Mass preparation, Benediction, and then another free period until bedtime. Confessions were heard during this period, and one might talk to Father Judge about a particular problem.

I talked to him about the house and my relationship to it, and told him the questions in my mind, one night.

Yes, in his opinion, it really was "worth it," he said. It really would do "some lasting good"—though I might never see it. It could change me, it ought to. In fact, he pointed out, if I did it for love of God, in humility and obedience, it should make me a saint. It would take a lifetime, for perfection is not achieved this day, but all our days. Our perfection consists in our continual striving for it. And so it went with all the questions.

I thought of his answers during the rest of the retreat, and by the time it ended I had accepted them. I don't know if it made things any easier, but anyway, it made things make sense.

18

After the retreat had ended I was talking to Marge Hughes about Father Meenan. He was her good friend too. She had visited him recently and suggested I be sure and do so before I went back home. I said I wanted to but couldn't afford it. She said that didn't matter and gave me my fare and Butch's. Then Jane O'Donnell, who had been keeping the house and work at Maryfarm going during the retreat as well as teaching the singing and otherwise helping with the retreat itself, suggested I call him and find out when I could go and see him.

Father Meenan was very surprised to hear my voice over the telephone, and delighted, he said, to learn that I was in New York. He said that he would be home Monday and Tuesday and for me to come either day, and bring Butch. That made me very happy, for I wanted to see him very much. St. Paul said to his spiritual children at Corinth: "For if you have ten thousand instructors in Christ, yet not many fathers. For in Christ Jesus, by the gospel, I have begotten you." So it is with Father Meenan, for it was through his example and teaching that I was born of God in the Church.

Another woman making the retreat offered to drive me back down to New York City, since it was on her way. Gratefully I accepted. It was quite a trip. The car caught fire due to a short circuit in some wires, and she just managed to get it off the busy highway. Then we had to find a garage and wait until the trouble was corrected. After that we had to stop and pick up her small daughter, whom she had left in the care of friends as I had left Butch.

At last we reached the city, at about eight-thirty in the evening. By the time I reached Aunt Marion's house, it was around nine o'clock. Butch was fast asleep on the couch where he had been waiting for me. I picked him up and tried to awaken him, but he only stirred a little. "Butchy Boy," I called him, "you don't know who's got you."

"Mother," he said drowsily, and settled back for a long sleep.

"Why don't you just stay here tonight?" Aunt Marion suggested. "There's room there on the couch. And you can go right over here to St. Charles' to church in the morning."

I was tired, and grateful for the suggestion. And in a little while I had joined Butch in slumber.

The next day Butch and I went to the Museum of Natural History, which he liked very much. When we had looked at the animals, I showed him the molded figures of a mother and child, the baby shown growing in the womb of the mother. He was interested and wanted to know if I had carried him so. I assured him I had and he marveled at this mystery.

"Isn't God wonderful to make our bodies so perfect," I commented, watching him. "See how He thought to make a mother so she could keep her baby so nobody could hurt it while it is too little? And how He made her so she could give him milk to drink when he is hungry?"

Butch agreed that this was wonderful. And the wonder of it satisfied his curiosity in these matters for a long while, so he did not ask me more than this.

That night our friend Emily Adams, who had been my "big sister" in nursing school, took us to Coney Island. She was a registered nurse now, and I was very proud of her. She did not have what we jokingly called in nursing "long sleevitis." (That meant that the new graduate's new status had gone to her head and filled her with a temporary—usually—pride and air of superiority over mere laymen and student nurses.) She was the same as ever—full of a deep sense of humor and an even deeper sense of concern for real human problems and human needs, and a living faith, though it was not my own. (She is an Anglican.) She was still a non-conformist with the courage to think and live according to her own convictions, without compromising them for the opinions of others. She dressed the way she liked to dress, and chose her friends because she liked them. Some were white, some colored as she is, some very poor, some upper-middle-class. Some were deeply religious; one of her best was an atheist.

I felt completely at home with her because her friendship left you free to be yourself. You did not have to strive to live up to, nor down to, a false self who only existed in her imagination, as you sometimes have to do for friends.

At Coney Island we played in the water a bit, then Butch rode the horses and took a few other rides alone. Emily rode a boat with him and I rode something like a big hoop that went over and over. We ate pizzas and candy apples and other indigestibles and Butch enjoyed it thoroughly and we enjoyed his enjoyment. Emily persuaded us to go on the Wonder Wheel with her. That is a very high wheel like a ferris wheel, only very much bigger, and with cars which don't merely swing but roll up and back on a track as the wheel turns over. Ugh! I didn't like that!

When we left Coney Island Emily bought Butch a toy and a cowboy hat, and one apiece for me to carry back to Denise's children. Butch went to sleep on the subway train going home, and Emily and I talked about our faiths and about nursing. We talked about the race problem, and finally about music. She promised to bring her guitar over to the Catholic Worker when I came back from Norwalk, Connecticut—where Father Meenan was. Then we would sing songs together, she said. I knew Betty Lou and the other women at the Catholic Worker would like that as much as I would.

Sunday, Butch and I went to Mass at the Eastern rite church, St. Michael's, to which I had gone so often when I lived in New York, and sung in the choir. It was good to be back. There were the tables set and the smell of coffee being made. There were Tess, and Jessie, and all the others whom I had missed so much. There, later, was Father Rogosh, smiling a welcome, and some others whose names I had forgotten, but whose faces were dearly familiar. I asked John if I might sing in the choir and he said yes. I knew I had not forgotten how, because very often in the sanatorium I had sung the whole of the people's responses and the hymns in my little copy of the Divine Liturgy to myself in the Slavonic because I loved to sing it. Even at Blessed Martin House, I sang parts from it and had tried to teach the larger children parts when I had time.

I have often thought there is something about the music and the ritual of the Byzantine rite that is much closer to the music and spirit of my own people than the music and ritual of the Roman rite. I had to learn to like Gregorian and learn to like the calmness and joyous austerity of the Mass I sing now several times a week, which is my own. But the warmth and richness of the other, the spontaneity of the responses, the generosity of the bows, found an answer in my own being that needed no learning. Perhaps the sadness and tortured melancholy of the Russian spirit, which Dostoyevsky, Tolstoi, and Chekhov describe so well, expresses itself best in Russian folk music and the Liturgy of the Church, as the spirit of the Negro is expressed best in the Negro spirituals and gospel songs; and perhaps there is between the two a kinship which bridges a continent and an ocean, each to find an echo in the other; for in both there is a searching that hopes against hope, a singing in the dark by faith, as if even the reprobate know there is nothing but God. But in the singing you can hear the darkness and follow the path of sadness under the joy, but the triumph of the joy over the sadness is truly triumphant, warm and glorious, in its richness and fullness, because it is unexpected.

But I am glad that our Mother, the Church, has both Eastern and Roman rites. It shows she is truly the mother of us all, so that whether I offer the Sacrifice according to the rubrics of my own rite or of one of the Eastern rites, it is still the same Sacrifice, the same Christ I offer with the whole Church, for we are all one in Christ.

After the Divine Liturgy, we had breakfast and Father Rogosh gave us a beautiful icon to take home with us, for Blessed Martin House.

Monday we went to Norwalk to see Father Meenan. Dorothy Day gave us our fare, though I told her Marge had already given it to us. "Oh, you'll need it, anyway," she said.

When we arrived and rang the bell Father answered the door himself. He looked the same, except his hair was thinner.

"Well, it's good to see you, and here's Butch," he greeted us, as he opened the door. "Come in."

We talked a long time about the retreat and about myself and Blessed Martin House mostly, but Father asked about a lot of friends in New York and sent messages back to them.

He was very interested in the house and was especially enthusiastic over our Bishop's approval. When I told him that Bishop Adrian had sent us a small check to help us, he said I really didn't realize how very much I had received.

"God is really with you," he told me. "He must be pleased with your work." He suggested that even though our Bishop had not asked for it, I send a report to him at least once a year, better twice, on the activities and progress of the house. I promised to do that, and thanked him for the suggestion. Then he reminded me not to take complacency at the visible progress we seemed to be making, nor yet fear adversity or apparent failure, or opposition from others.

"Unless the seed falling into the ground die," he reminded me again, "it remains alone. But if it dies, it brings forth much fruit." I must not fear these things, nor suffering, for these too are a part of God's providence and of His love, he said. Once more, it was the folly of the

cross, God using our weakness and littleness and sufferings and failures, to do strong things, big things, joyous
things in His Name and for His glory. He suggested a
few books I could profit by reading, and I promised to
read them if I could get them.

Then we walked around the grounds of the seminary
outside. Some young seminarians were swimming, and
some boys about twelve or fourteen years old, who had
come up to see what a seminary was like. They took
Butch in hand and fed him watermelon and played with
him in the water, while Father and I walked and talked
about him and about some personal problems of my own.

When we had finished our walk, we found Butch in
the driver's seat of the big Greyhound bus which had
brought the boys up. He was trying to turn the wheel
and honking the horn. He was a truly happy little boy
and feeling big and important. He offered to drive us
into New York, but Father Meenan and I both declined.
After much persuasion, at last he agreed to let the driver
have his seat and the boys go home, and to go in with us
for supper.

The meal was very good, and when it ended Father
drove us down to the railroad station and waited with
us for our train. When it approached, he gave us an
envelope with money in it for our fare.

I had to laugh. "Oh, no, Father, this is the third fare
I've gotten for this trip. God must really have wanted
me to come. But I won't take it, because Marge and
Dorothy have already given it to me."

But Father insisted. "Take it anyway. A true Catholic
worker doesn't refuse money from friends. Use it for
the house or whatever you want to. You'll need it."

So the third "fare" went into my pocket to be used for myself or Blessed Martin House, whichever need came up first.

The next day, I went over to Harlem Hospital to get a pneumo-thorax treatment. I stopped by to say hello to some of the girls who had been students with me, and to my godmother, Miss Spady.

Later Emily came over and we sang songs while she played the guitar. We sang folk songs and Negro spirituals, and she sang some calypso alone, because I did not know any. The men in the breadline and those in the kitchen getting ready to serve them listened and showed visibly their enjoyment. The women in the women's house came down to listen. So did Dorothy and Betty Lou. We sang "The Cowboy's Lament," "Jimcrow," "Barbara Allen," "Jericho," "Go Down, Moses," and many others. Emily sang "Linstead Market," "Brown Skin Girl Go Mind Bab-bee" and several others. She had a way of lowering her head intently over her instrument, then raising it suddenly in her song, that made her seem wholly free and a part of her music. When at last she had finished, some of the men and women came out to thank her. She had given us all a moment of real pleasure that would grow with the memory of it.

When the time came for us to leave for Washington, she went with us to the train station, and gave us money to help us on the way. She promised to come and see us as soon as possible.

In Washington we went directly to Friendship House. We stayed the week-end, and one of the volunteers took us to the Museum of Art. Butch still wore his brace, and I was happily surprised to find in the museum, strollers and wheelchairs provided for the physically handicapped, to make their tour less tiring. A guard went and found one for us, so Butch rode in style through the museum.

Early the next morning we drove with others to the farm in Burnley, Virginia, Maria Laach Farm. I was glad to see Father O'Keefe again, who was to give the other course. I had met him in Memphis where he had come to visit Jim. And that meeting was associated in my mind with the double delight of having him talk to our study group and of having Jim bring him. At first I had feared that Jim would never forgive me the house, because of some of his friends' opposition to it, nor understand what I had never been able to explain without speaking un-kindly of his friends. But he had not only come to visit the house himself once or twice, while he was in Mem-phis, but he had obtained donations for it from others on at least two occasions and had suggested Father O'Keefe as a speaker for the Outer Circle meetings. Father O'Keefe had been a good speaker too, on the liturgy and the liturgical movement. I thought of all of that as I greeted him warmly on Maria Laach Farm.

I was also pleased to find I already knew two of the summer students: Kathleen from Caritas in New Orleans, and Lois, one of their volunteers. I had never before met Charlie Slack, who was in charge of the farm, except by letter, but I liked him at once. Then there were three other volunteers from Friendship House, whom I also liked at once. It promised to be a fruitful and happy week, and it was.

Father talked about race with a special stress on the value of the liturgy in overcoming prejudice, as people worshipped together the One God in His One Church. I spoke about the race problem as a Negro and a Catholic, drawing examples and references freely from my own experiences, particularly at Blessed Martin House. I explained how I had found Father's theme practical for myself in Memphis, attending the "white" church in the parish in which I live out of principle.

I explained how at first some of the white parishioners were cool, though none openly discourteous, and I refused to see their coolness. I went because it was Our Father's House, whether they would admit our kinship or not, to offer His Sacrifice with Him and with them, and to receive Him as food for my body and my soul.

They did not have a real choir. There was a small school then, and a few children sang the Mass, often very weakly. I began singing with them, remaining in my own seat, however, and not going up with them into the choir stalls. By the following year there was no school any more. The attendance was so small, since it was a Negro neighborhood and few white children lived there, that it was no longer practical to have a school for white children. The two Catholic colored schools were very crowded, and many people wondered why the school was not given to colored children. Some hoped and believed that it would be, but it was not. I don't know why. But however that may be, there was no longer anybody to lead the children in singing, except for the special big feast days when a Sister came from another school to teach them. At least three times every week there was a high Mass for the day and the children sang it alone, often making many mistakes.

One day I suggested to one of the little girls whom I knew because she had sometimes come to Blessed Martin House to our parties, and whose brothers and cousins were frequent visitors there, that they listen to me and follow me in singing.

"We can't hear you good down there all the time," she explained.

"Then I'll come up there," I offered, and she seemed pleased at the thought of having me. So did the other little girls.

After that I sang the Mass with them all the time, except on Sunday. The first time the organist came and found me there (I had been singing several weeks then, for we mostly sing without an organ) she seemed a little surprised, but not very. She was used to seeing me at church by then, and used to hearing me singing downstairs. She didn't say anything, though. She didn't even speak. She acted as if I were not there.

But I continued coming and continued being quietly friendly, and after a while she began to speak, and finally she began to smile and seemed to welcome my coming. It had taken a long time and a lot of patience, but at last I was accepted and sang even on Sundays.

Now I felt truly a part of that church and the people were mostly friendly. If some still did not speak, a few others went out of their way to do so.

In other talks during the week I told of other ways we tried to combat the racial problem at Blessed Martin House.

"I do have an advantage that most of you do not have," I explained. "That is, in being both a Negro and a Southerner. Ordinary people can understand why I would be concerned with the problem on purely natural grounds. I have a son and parents and brothers who will benefit or suffer according to how the South develops, just as I will myself. A white Southerner working on the problem in the South has an even greater advantage, because he is one of them, no matter how different and radical his ideas are. His is 'old man so-and-so's son' and entitled, according to Southern loyalties, to definite rights, and the freedom to believe as he likes and act very much in accordance with what he believes. You Northerners are going to have a hard time working on this if you come South, because in many places they are still fighting the Civil War. You are, and always will be, Yankees, damn Yankees, interfering.

"But, of course, being a Negro working in the South has its definite disadvantages too. The law was not made for me. They have a thousand and one ways of reminding me of that; that this *is* a 'white man's country.' I live on sufferance, not by right. And it is hard for me to be regarded simply as a person.

"I try to break that down by forming personal friendships with the members of the Outer Circle, giving them a chance to live up to the principles which they say they hold, without forcing them to go any further than they can. Some go all the way and accept me and my family as friends and treat us as friends, despite what others in their own race say or think. Maybe they are called 'Nigger lovers.' They never have told me if they are. I imagine some are. But they are willing to risk that and more because they believe what they say they do about the Mystical Body and because we are friends.

"So, the first and hardest step in making friends, is providing normal situations where colored and white people can work or live together as equals, as brothers, and learn to be friends. It is hard for most people, I think, to love, concretely, an abstract 'Negro race,' with a love that takes risks or makes sacrifices. It is somewhat easier to have that kind of love for this person, then this community, then this people.

"It is hard, but the idea is to get white volunteers used to the idea of serving Negroes, when they have been used to thinking of Negroes as the servants, and to replace a sort of paternal condescension or tolerance with friendship, or with a real Christian charity, in the true sense of charity.

"And white prejudice isn't the only enemy you'll find, but you have to add to that Negro indifference and fear, yes, and prejudice. And unthought-out actions of belligerence from some Negro groups which have resulted in a violent antagonism, on one hand, and the servility and obsequiousness of some Negroes on the other hand, which has made it seem to some white people that we are content with what we have, or incapable of anything better. Those points are a bit ticklish, though, for white people to handle, and probably belong to us who are Negroes to solve."

The group and Father O'Keefe seemed very much interested in that, and we had many discussions on various ways of breaking down racial prejudice. We all agreed that we've got to start with ourselves, and we must act out of motives of love.

One night we had a panel discussion on the problem. Four were on the panel to talk about the need of colored children for a Catholic education. The rest of us were supposed to be white parents questioning the panel's aim to have colored children admitted to the school our children attended. It was very real, but since it was make-believe, it was funny too. We were really prejudiced. One dark-colored girl drew herself up and sniffed audibly. "Miss———," she said, "isn't it true that colored people smell bad? I don't want my children associating with people who smell bad."

The panelist patiently explained that color had no odor, but that anyone who had bad hygienic habits would smell bad. "It is the aim of our schools, among other things, to teach good hygienic habits. I have known many colored people; in fact, I have colored friends, and I assure you they don't smell bad."

"But isn't it true," I objected, "that Negro children are mostly delinquent, that they have low moral standards?" (This was an objection I had frequently heard myself.) "I'm not prejudiced, but after all, I want to watch the environment of my children. I wouldn't want my children associating with people like that, and I have five children here."

The panelist commended me on my family and pointed out that there are juvenile delinquents among colored people just as there are juvenile delinquents among white people. "It is not the color," she explained patiently. "If your children had been forced to live in crowded tenements in back alleys in the slums, they might be delinquents too. We want to give these children an opportunity to know a better way of life."

And so on and on it went, each of us offering objections we had heard and sometimes having them answered by the panelist and occasionally answering our own objections. We all learned a lot and were all better prepared, in theory at least, to meet situations of prejudice that would surely arise in our various apostolates.

In between conferences we helped with the work of the farm, and went walking or wading. Butch especially liked to play in the water. We had picnics and toasted marshmallows and sang folksongs over a campfire. We drank beer or coffee in the house before an open fireplace on a chilly night and sang more folksongs. When we grew tired we said Compline and went to bed.

Every morning began with a dialogue or sung Mass and Prime. During the day there was, in place of the little hours—Tierce, Sext and None—the Rosary, and every evening ended with Compline.

It was a fruitful and full study week and I was sorry when it ended. But Butch and I remained over another week just for the rest of it, the peacefulness. That was our "vacation." We explored the woods and ate walnuts and fished for days without ever catching a thing. One day we went in to the state sanatorium for me to get my "pneumo," and while there we went around the state university. Someone pointed out Edgar Allen Poe's room to me and I was fascinated, because he has always been a favorite of mine. At the "san" the doctor told me, "If you were my patient I would have discontinued your pneumo long ago." He suggested that I tell my doctor to discontinue it. I could hardly resist a smile at that. I could just see myself telling Doctor Alley or his assistant, Dr. Cole, who usually treated me, anything of the kind. I might ask when, and hope tomorrow, but every time I had asked he answered vaguely (and still does), "Maybe in a couple of years."

"Oh, well," I consoled myself, "perhaps obeying your doctor's orders and decisions is a part of the virtues of holy obedience."

All too soon that week ended also, and it was time to go home. Bertha McGrauer, from Caritas, had driven Kathleen and Lois up from New Orleans and then gone on to visit her family in Pennsylvania. Now she returned for them to take them home. She offered to give us a ride back as far as Birmingham, Alabama. That was a very welcome surprise, and would save considerably on our train fare, since it is only about seven dollars from Birmingham to Memphis, against thirty-one dollars from Washington to Memphis.

They had a big station wagon, so it was not very crowded. Bertha was the only one of us who could drive, and it made it very tiring for her. Otherwise, I think, we all enjoyed the trip. We carried lunches, but we stopped on the way to eat in drive-in restaurants, taking our food outside in the car in order to stay together.

When night came we had the problem of finding shelter. We had crossed the Mason-Dixon line into No Man's Land, and there are few places across the line for Negro tourists, and none for mixed groups such as ours. On principle we did not want to separate, so finally we hit on an idea. We looked for tourist camps with individual cabins and secluded entrances. When we saw one, Butch and I lay down with our heads covered and snored. Lois is brown, but an Oriental brown that can pass for white when with white people, and she sat up and a little back. Bertha and Kathleen talked to the manager, and he rented us two cabins, and Bertha said we would not need anything during the night.

Bertha drove into the garage, and we crept out of the car, feeling and looking like criminals, but criminals who had no conscience about their crime. We laughed and joked as we stealthily made our way inside. Bertha, Lois, and Kathleen took one cabin and Butch and I took the other. I gave him a bath and took a shower myself and finished the Little Office of Our Lady. Butch said his prayers also and went to bed. He was asleep in a moment. I was not long in joining him, and we both slept comfortably, although once I had to get up and throw a coat over us in the night when it became chilly. Of course we did not dare ring for a blanket.

Early the next morning before anyone else was awake, we crept out, a little defiantly this time. We were rested, and there was nothing anyone could do now but make us leave, and that we were doing anyway.

"Well, some Southerner can say he slept in a bed once that a nigger slept in," I said, laughing, and they joined me.

We found a church and went to Mass and received Our Lord, then continued on our way.

The rest of the trip was uneventful. The others left us in Birmingham at the train station. They reminded me of my promise to visit them again in New Orleans, and I tried to persuade Bertha to pay a visit to Memphis.

Butch and I had several hours to wait until train time, so we went for a walk. We visited a church near the depot, then went to a café for dinner. The food was good and the price reasonable. We both enjoyed it. After that we went to a movie, a treat Butch especially liked. We left the movie in time to catch the train and soon we were sleeping in the hard coach seats, speeding on our way to Memphis.

19

THERE WERE SO MANY SMALL CHILDREN IN THE NURSERY at Blessed Martin House, when we came back from New York, that there was no longer enough time to plan a program for the larger children in the Community Center, nor was there anyone to execute it, if planned. I was still the only one on the house staff, unless the children's mothers and the volunteers could be counted so. The mothers were surprisingly impatient with the larger children, for the most part, and wholly without sympathy for, or understanding of, their problems. They wanted to get through with the work and go home. They did not want to play with the children and were irritated when the latter were noisy or when they messed up the house. There were still few volunteers, and these could come only in the daytime, but the Community Center was open only in the evening after school and at night. Bob had gone away to teach school. The girls at Sienna, who had been coming, first were on vacation and later were so involved in classes and other activities in their senior year, that they seldom came any more.

Gradually, most of the larger children stopped coming, except to the parties, which became rarer and rarer as expenses at the house increased and donations decreased. Several members of the Outer Circle moved out of town. One white mother called me to tell me not to call her daughter or ask her to come and help me. She (the daughter) had been a faithful volunteer. Now she came no more.

At the same time, the "family" grew in the house itself. A group called and asked me to give temporary shelter to a twelve-year-old girl whose father was threatening to kill her whole family, and she came to stay with us for a few weeks. Her mother came and told me her version of the family squabble. Her father came and told me his (which sounded to me much more likely, though I spoke my opinion aloud only to Denise). In the end the parents resolved their difficulties and the child went home with her father.

Meanwhile, Father Coyne learned that he was being transferred to Louisiana. All his parishioners hated to see him go, but none of them, I think, any more than we did, though we were not in his parish. He had been a good moderator and had helped us over many a rough spot and in countless ways. He had encouraged me when I most needed encouragement. "Go ahead," he had said, when I had been ready to give up the whole thing. He had contributed spiritually to the house by his Masses said for us, and materially by the collections he had taken up for us.

I went with Rosemary to the farewell party given for him at the rectory by his parishioners, and we carried him a gift. He promised not to forget us in his new mission and to visit us when he could.

While he was getting ready to leave and after he left, I went to see several priests who had been interested in Blessed Martin House for a long time and who had helped in various ways. I wanted to ask their permission to send their names to the Bishop for his appointment of a new moderator. There was Father Robert, the pastor of our parish; Father Murphy, my friend from Isolation Hospital and my confessor; there was Father Hostettler; and later the new priest at St. Anthony's, Father Sheedy. Except for the latter, whom I did not know, all had shown some special interest in the house and seemed to me to have a genuine understanding of the real spirit behind it. That was especially evident, I felt, in Father Murphy, who had worked as a volunteer in Friendship House while in the seminary, and I especially hoped that he would be appointed. But I would have been pleased to have any of them as spiritual director.

Father Sheedy, the new priest at St. Anthony, gave his permission with an understandable reluctance. He was new in Memphis and unfamiliar with the situation, the problem, and the house itself. The others all said they would be glad to have me send their names.

As soon as I had talked to the last one about it, I wrote to Bishop Adrian and told him our need and en-closed the names, asking him to appoint one, stating a slight preference for Father Murphy.

In a few days, Father Murphy and I both received letters from our Bishop, notifying us of Father's appoint-ment, subject to the approval of his pastor—who made no objection. In the letter to me Bishop Adrian had enclosed a check for the house as well. I was full of joy at that, and worked all that day singing the song of the Cherubim from the Byzantine rite, and the Kyrie from the Mass

Cum Jubilo, and the Gloria from Montani's *Missa Brevis*, because my joy had to find expression, and for me song is the most natural way of expressing it. Ida caught my spirit, and she too sang, off and on, all day. Even Denise, who was very unhappy those days, seemed to share the joy of the moment.

I repeated a phrase of the letter to Ida, laughing. "He says of the check, 'Perhaps this will be of some help at this time.' *Perhaps!* That is a master understatement! Now we can pay our rent and know our family has a place for another month."

I looked around lovingly at "our family," and the house we had to rent because we could do no better.

Often during the day then there were twenty-five or thirty children in the nursery, and the one big room had become more and more crowded. Denise and her children had our room, so Butch and I slept in his youth bed in the nursery together. Denise and Bubble, her son, slept in a small bed together, and Roy slept in his crib in the room with them. In addition to these beds we had to keep all our clothing (all five of us) in that small room, and all the bedding, etc., for the house. The telephone was there too, and there was just space between the trunk and beds to walk to the telephone, because the whole room only measured nine by twelve feet.

St. Thomas the cat, familiarly known as Tom Cat, kept the rats out, but we could still hear them scampering about in the walls and under the floors and in the ceiling at night. We heard them fighting and squealing in the room behind us, where the woman who rented the beauty shop next door slept occasionally. In the other room the cook-stove sat on a small platform, partly partitioned off from the rest of the room by sagging boards. Whenever it rained, up from the rotten boards a musty odor rose, like the stench of something long dead. Don said it was from an old sewer which ran underground in that part of the city. It may have been. Anyway, nothing could kill the odor. We poured down buckets of soapy lye water, and Pine-Sol and Lysol, but none were very effective. After a while we learned to live with it.

Always too, there was the battle against roaches. They were in the walls, behind the sinks, and in the floors. In the day, when we sprayed, they hid, but they crept out at night, big black ones with wings. Butch was terrified of them and would cry until he was sure the "bug" was dead.

And the plumbing was always out of order. Our landlord gave his tenants as little as he could and charged as much as he could. We paid seventy-five dollars a month and those living in the other rooms paid eight dollars a week, despite the small size of the rooms and the falling plaster and the screenless windows. When something had to be fixed, he got any unlicensed carpenter or plumber to do the work who would do it cheaply. So the work was often done so badly that the "repair" only lasted a few days. Then when a new complaint was made, he would go into a fierce tantrum which frightened the other tenants—who sometimes couldn't pay their rent anyway—and made them drop the complaint. He didn't frighten me, though, and I soon learned that I could get him to repair a good many things promptly by complaining a few days before rent was due and refusing to pay unless the repairs were attended to first. He didn't like that at all, but, finding me adamant, he acquiesced with as bad grace as possible.

I remember one day in particular (though that was

before Denise came). I had been down to St. Bridget's, making a visit to Our Lord in the Blessed Sacrament. When I came back, just as I stepped in the door of the room where Butch and I slept, the gas came on under the hot water tank with a "whoosh!" and set the rug beneath on fire. I was frightened, but I managed to put it out, singeing my eyebrows in the process. I called the Memphis Gas and Water Division Service department, and they sent a man to cut the gas off. He came and cut it off and informed me that it must not be turned on again until the tank was moved into the other room. It was not supposed to be in a bedroom, he said, but would have to be in the kitchen or toilet.

He left me wondering how I could persuade our landlord to move the tank. By this time the babies were waking up. I didn't have much time to think about it then. Instead, I began taking them out of bed. Some were in play pens, sleeping. These pens I folded and put away. I went outside to get the clothes from the line.

Suddenly a child ran outside to me. "Miss Helen! Miss Helen!" she cried excitedly, "the house is falling down!"

I ran inside with her. Where a baby had been sleeping a few minutes before, there was now a big chunk of plaster, the size of a large platter, and lots of little pieces. In the ceiling there was a big gaping hole where it had been.

"Oh, my God!" I thought to myself. "If the baby had been there, it might have been killed." And the thought filled me with coldness. I was deeply grateful to God, though, for averting the tragedy.

I cleaned up the mess with Ida's help and the help of another volunteer. I still felt a little sick and afraid.

Too much had happened at once and I could feel all my old doubts and fears stirring within me. I felt terribly alone and everything in me was dark.

But there was still work to be done. I diapered the babies and cleaned the children for the evening. The older children came in and quarrelled and played until about nine-thirty. Then Ida helped me clean up after them and went home. I mopped the floor and went to the front to lock the door.

When I came back to go to bed, I saw a steady stream of dirty brown water pouring down from the hole in the ceiling. Underneath, the newly mopped floor gleamed dully in a brown puddle of water. I took the mop again and looked balefully at our statue of Blessed Martin as I wiped up the water.

"You've got a nasty sense of humor," I told him spitefully, but with a lightened heart. For some reason, I felt better. I couldn't explain why. It was just too much, I guess. Before, there had been in me only fear and darkness. Now it had reached the ridiculous, or so it seemed to me, and in me faith and hope had revived.

"I'm not afraid of you," I said to no one in particular. I put the mop down and turned off the lights. I said my prayers and climbed into bed beside Butch. In an instant I was sleeping.

But such problems as these made it evident that we would have to find another place as soon as possible, not for rent but for sale. It should be in that same parish and neighborhood, because both the need and the help were there. This pastor, these neighbors, and the grocers at these neighborhood stores, were friendly and helpful. The people who lived in this neighborhood were the kind of people I wanted to reach at Blessed Martin House.

I started looking for houses for sale. Father Murphy encouraged me. He understood the need. I told the members of the Outer Circle that I was going to buy a house. The practical ones wanted to know how much there was in the bank for Blessed Martin House.

"We have about five dollars. I'm not sure exactly. Not more than ten, I know."

They thought I was joking. Some thought I was a little mad, or impossibly impractical and presumptuous.

"If God wants us to have a house, He will send us the money," I insisted. "It would be cheaper than trying to pay this rent, and we'd have something to show for it."

I listened to more lectures on prudence and being practical, but Father Murphy upheld me. He said, "We should be more willing to trust in Divine Providence for our needs." I thanked God for Father Murphy.

All the while Denise was becoming more and more interested in the Outer Circle and the work of the house itself. She marveled at our trust, when Father talked about Providence, although she could not share it. As the days passed, I became convinced that something great in her own soul might depend on whether or not we succeeded in getting the house. It was as if something in her own spirit had been so long sleeping that it had seemed dead. Now it was stirring, and it needed this one more thing to waken it to a new life.

I watched the real estate section of the papers for Negro property for sale. I called several realtors, asking them to call me if they wanted to sell property within a certain area (bounded by four streets which enclosed a great number of houses, all within walking distance from St. Bridget's church). That was a crowded neighborhood, and people weren't trying to sell because of the comfortable rents on old, run-down property, often beyond repair. But at last I heard of two houses for sale, both within three blocks of the church.

One was beautiful, a two-story brick with a nice yard and hedges in front and a fence behind. There were about fourteen or more rooms. It appeared to be in good repair and was in a neighborhood of comfortable houses like itself. The down payment was twenty-five hundred dollars and the notes were ninety dollars a month.

The other was small, six rooms, a small yard with no fence. The ground was hard and dusty, as if the soil was long emptied of all its elements. There was no plumbing inside, but there were a hydrant and a toilet outside in the yard. The wallpaper was dirty and torn, and the plaster was falling down in many places. Some of the floors were sunken in places, or rotten underneath. The place looked as if it had never been painted, but most of the siding still looked good and strong. The windows were in pretty good condition, and so, said the present tenants, was the roof.

The house was in an alley, a block off Beale Street, in the rear, in a crowded neighborhood of houses like itself, poor and run-down. There were lots of dirty children playing in the alley, and grown-ups sitting on the porches in the cool air, talking. But they spoke as I passed them. (The big house had been quiet, and I had seen no one in the neighborhood at all. Perhaps all were working.) The price was four thousand dollars, with four hundred down and forty dollars a month.

I took Father Murphy to see both houses. He liked the big house with its yard, but not the neighborhood. It was getting away from the really poor, he said. He wondered if these people would come to us as freely there as they did in our present location. When he heard the price and the amount of down payment and the notes, he made a face and exclaimed aloud. He thought we should look further.

When he saw the little house, he was enthusiastic. "This is it," he said. "It really is in the right neighborhood." Secretly, I agreed with him. I had felt a great and inexplicable attraction to the place myself, but I did not want to influence him unduly, so I pointed out the defects I had noted.

"It would need painting and a lot of repair," I pointed out. "There is no bathroom or inside plumbing. The plaster is falling in places, and I don't know if we'd ever get grass to grow. We'd need a fence to keep the children in, and worst of all is the alley. It would keep the children off the street, but it's hard walking and would be harder driving. People would have to really want to see us to find us here, I mean people in the Outer Circle—people like that."

"But couldn't we have a sign, or something like that? I think we could get volunteers to help us fix the place up—we could ask some of the men who have been interested in the house. It looks like a good buy. But we could talk it over with some of the members of the group."

I carried several other people down to see the house, and reactions ranged from enthusiasm to real horror. Some members of the Outer Circle, who had been members of the study group before and who had helped the house in many ways, were enthusiastic about all but the plumbing. They were afraid this alone would run into a thousand dollars. If I could get that done reasonably, though, they believed the place would be a good buy. Some other members disliked the neighborhood and thought the house beyond repair. Bob Nieman, a new volunteer and an engineer, thought the house had possibilities but would cost much to repair. One or two other members believed they knew plumbers who would do the job at a reasonable price and thought men from the Knights of Columbus or the St. Vincent de Paul Society might help with the repairs. Still another volunteer told me that she was sure few white people would come to see us in "that dirty alley," and let me know she would be one of the many, and not of the few. She disapproved thoroughly.

Meanwhile I received a letter from Dorothy Day, saying that she was coming to see me. Several times in the past, she had promised to come on a visit, but each time she had been prevented from doing so. I was glad she was coming now instead. She could see the need and the houses and advise me. I would know that her advice came from years of experience in being poor, of loving the poor and living with the poor and sharing the problems and precariousness that are a part of the lives of the poor. Her prudence would not be that of merely human considerations, but would, I was sure, be guided by supernatural motives of charity. So I could listen in good conscience and follow it.

I was glad for another reason as well. I wanted her to talk to the members of the study group and volunteers. I wanted them to hear from her, and see in her, something of the real spirit of the Catholic Worker movement, which I wanted to continue in Memphis. I express myself so badly, and there is so much that cannot be expressed in words, that I hoped they could understand, from her account, something of the history and working of other houses of hospitality in other places, something of the real spirit of Blessed Martin House.

When I began calling friends of the house to invite them, some wanted her to speak to other groups. C.B.C. (Christian Brothers) would like her, and Sienna; Father Sheedy wanted her for St. Anthony's. I promised, for her, that she would speak to these groups, and planned a time for her to speak at the house, hoping that she would be able to speak at all these places.

Dorothy was ill on the day she was supposed to come, so she did not arrive until late in the evening on the day before she was supposed to speak. She was very tired, so she had supper and went to bed. The next day we went down to St. Bridget's for Mass together, then came back to breakfast. She helped to diaper and feed the babies, and feed the older children, and doled out the cod-liver oil and candy.

Father Murphy came over and she met him, and he drove us out to Catholic High for pictures.

That evening before she was to talk at Blessed Martin House, she went down to the peace of St. Bridget's— for Blessed Martin House was not very restful, as there was no privacy and the children were many and noisy— to think.

While she was at church, Denise, Ida, and I began to clean up and put out the chairs for the people we had invited. Mary Lee and Mary Lou, our big little helpers from the Community Center, put cookies on plates, got the cups out for coffee, and helped in other such ways. Several members of the Outer Circle brought more cookies, or milk, or coffee. Father Robert loaned us more chairs from St. Bridget's.

The people began to come. Almost all the members of the Outer Circle were there, and some strangers. There were students from Sienna and C.B.C. There were several priests and Christian Brothers. There were volunteers from the house, even the one who had threatened not to help us any more or come to see us, if we bought the house in the alley.

Dorothy spoke. She talked about our unity in God, and of our obligations to each other in Him. She talked about poverty and the Catholic Worker and Blessed Martin House. She made an appeal for us, for volunteers and other help. She talked about the obligations of the rich, and quoted in that regard some strong words of Our Lord, beginning: "Woe unto you rich . . . you have had your reward." She quoted Peter Maurin's reminder that we take with us when we die only what we have given away, in Our Lord's name, while we live.

I watched the faces of those who listened. Some were deeply interested and became more and more thoughtful or alive. Some were closed and dead and remained so. Some grew red and angry, and I could see the effort it cost these people not to speak until she had finished. Some never understood. The colored people were awed and unbelieving at all this from a white woman. There was new hope in some of their faces, and a nameless delight. These would never forget what she had said. For one moment they had been lifted by her out of our little world.

As soon as she had taken her seat, the questions began, some angry and hot.

"Is there something particularly holy about poverty and dirt, or rats and roaches? Does God stop loving a man because he works and saves his money to provide for wants and needs of his family, or is there something sinful about being rich? Doesn't charity begin at home?"

"No, there is nothing particularly holy about dirt and rats and roaches. But there may be something very unholy about the way we regard those who suffer from these things. The safety of the rich lies in almsgiving. We must give until we become the blessed. Blessed are the poor. Christ came to make the rich poor and the poor holy, Eric Gill said. When the Sadducees and Pharisees asked St. John the Baptist 'What must we do?' he answered, 'Let him who has two coats give to him who has none,' and with food likewise. Unquestioning sharing, unquestioning love.

"We must die to live, we must be pruned to bear fruit. We want to be free of responsibility except for our own. Yes, charity begins at home, but we are also our brother's keeper; we talk too much of our own homes, our own children.

"The Christian life is full of paradoxes. St. Thomas said that a certain amount of goods are necessary to lead a good life, and we are always talking about voluntary poverty. But ten million doses of sleeping pills will be taken tonight, and over seven million dollars worth of alcohol. There is money for coffee, movies, cosmetics, cigarettes, and many other things we could do without, that we could share with the poor."

"Doesn't the Catholic Worker encourage shiftlessness and laziness by feeding and sheltering people who won't help themselves? Don't you make people content with destitution by glorifying it, and take away their ambition to better themselves?"

Dorothy denied this. "No. Peter Maurin used to say that we must make the kind of society in which it is easier for people to be good.

"One needs to be happy to be good, and one needs to be good in order to be happy. One needs Christians to make a Christian social order and one needs a Christian social order in order to raise Christians. The paradox again. Such as dying to live. No one pretends it is a simple matter. It is all very hard to understand. The Christian must live in time and eternity, living with the long view, yet living most intensely at the moment. We are here to restore love, *caritas,* to the world, to overcome hatred with love. To receive charity and to give it is to practice loving."

"Aren't your ideas about the social order more Communist than Catholic?"

"No. We need always to remember that it is *atheistic* Communism which we oppose, but as for economic Communism—it is a system which has worked admirably in religious orders for two thousand years. The bishops once stated that many of the social aims of the Communist are Christian aims and must be worked for by Catholics. In our parishes and communities we should have credit unions, maternity guilds, and insurance benefit societies which would reach God's poorest. If we are trying to see Christ in our neighbor, we must see to his dignity, his worth, his position as a son of God. And to do this, it is not enough just to help out in an emergency. It is necessary to build a society where people are able by their work to sustain themselves, but also by mutual aid, to bear one another's burdens, when by sickness or accident men are unable to work."

The questions and answers continued until the lateness of the hour made it necessary to bring the meeting to a close. We all said Compline together and the others left. We cleaned the house and went to bed. Mother, Denise and Rosemary were very thoughtful. They had not heard anyone speak like this before.

While she was there, Dorothy spoke to the students at Sienna, C.B.C., and St. Anthony's. Except for C.B.C., where the talk included more about the Negro problem and pacifism, the talks were basically the same as that made at the house.

We had dinner with Linda Johns one day, and she was very much impressed with Dorothy's personality, with her sincerity and humility; but she did not agree with her; she could not understand her. She had seen the angry faces too, and she believed that more harm than good had been accomplished by the talk, because it had antagonized some who she thought were sincerely interested in the Negro and the poor. She was afraid of it. She did not think the controversy it had started would be good for the house.

The Negroes who had heard Dorothy at the house or at St. Anthony's were all very enthusiastic, as were most of those who only heard about it. But Richard was not. He never came to any of the Outer Circle meetings nor as a volunteer, but he called me over the telephone occasionally or dropped by the house to tell me how useless and hopeless he thought the work was at Blessed Martin House.

He was still wholly practical, and refused to see any prudence at all in trusting God's Providence for our material needs, nor use nor hope in our flouting or ignoring the unjust racial customs and restrictions around us.

"You just can't do these things down here," he was careful to keep me reminded. And when he had heard about Dorothy's talk, "You just can't talk like that down here."

"We are doing them. We are saying them," was always

my reply. "I'm a Dominican. Our motto is 'Truth.' If she said anything that was false or heretical, show me the error. If it was Truth, why should we be afraid to speak it aloud?"

He argued all around this. But the basis of his arguments was fear, and a glaringly false idea of humility that insulted the dignity of men, especially of our race. It is the same combination of fear and false humility that has made some Negro leaders insist, wrongly, that "The colored people are not looking for equality, but for justice" —as if there could be justice without equality in the sense we are using the word.

I was sorry he could not have heard Dorothy for himself. Perhaps she could have convinced him, whereas I could not.

Father Murphy and I took Dorothy to see both of the houses we were considering. She liked the big one too, because it was big and clean and beautiful, but she agreed that the neighborhood of the smaller was better. She wished with us that we could have found something better in that neighborhood but saw the possibilities of this if it were fixed up.

"If it's God's will that you have something better, you'll get it," she assured me with a calm confidence. "But you need a house."

We talked more about it at lunch over at my mother's house with Father Murphy and Brother Raphael. Brother Raphael promised that we would get some help from some of the boys at C.B.C., who would be interested in the work of repairing the little house, if we bought it. Several had seemed greatly interested in the house after Dorothy spoke. She had made them angry for a moment, but she had made them think, too. They had been awakened to a much fuller consciousness of their obligations as Catholics, because of that thought.

At last it was time for her to go. She embraced Denise warmly and gave her some money to get something she might want especially when the baby was born.

That simple gesture of love on her part served finally to crack the hard shell of distrust and hate and bitterness Denise had built around herself toward what had seemed to her a cold and unfriendly world since the tragic death of her mother in a fire many years before. At last the real Denise shone through, or the spirit of Christ in her, which had lain so patiently in His tomb fashioned of fear and distrust and sealed with the stone of suspicion. Here was His new Resurrection.

What was it that Dorothy herself had written once in one of her columns, "On Pilgrimage"? "Love in practice is a harsh and dreadful thing, compared to love in dreams. It reaches down, and like the sword of the spirit, it reaches down to the very marrow of our bones. But to receive charity and to give it, is to practice loving. We are accounted worthy to suffer for Christ in this dread struggle to learn loving."

This simple act of charity, expressed in a gesture and a kiss to a mother who was lonely and poor and miserable, summed up all she had been saying in her speaking in Memphis. Like the sword of the spirit, it had cut away the old man and slowly the new began to grow forth.

After we left Denise, Dorothy and I went, with Father Murphy driving us, to the train. The students at the schools had given her money to show their appreciation of her coming and speaking to them. She gave that to me, for the house, to pay some of the bills. And as we said goodbye, she promised to send me the down payment for the little house, and to put an appeal in *The Catholic Worker* for us. She promised to visit us again too.

"God's grace is truly in her," Father Murphy said as we watched the train go. I could only assent. My heart was full.

"Thank you, Peter Maurin. Thank you, Blessed Martin. I guess you want your house."

20

A FEW DAYS AFTER DOROTHY LEFT, I RECEIVED A CHECK from the *Catholic Worker* for four hundred dollars for the down payment on the new house. Shortly afterwards, the paper printed Dorothy's appeal for the house and many other people, friends of the *Catholic Worker*, sent us checks, large and small, to help pay for the house.

A girl in the Outer Circle called to tell me that her mother, who was in the real estate business, wanted to handle all the details of the purchase for me. That in itself meant much, but another detail made it mean much more: this mother was the same woman who, only a few months before, had called me and asked me not to call her daughter any more, nor ask her to come down to help me at the house. Now she herself was offering to help.

She handled all the details of the purchase and was able to get the house five hundred dollars cheaper than the price I had been given. She gave us her commission on the sale, eighty dollars. That was another saving. She had not liked the house nor the location, but she was very happy later because she had been able to help us, and she liked the house better when it appeared a bargain.

We could not move in or start repairs until the tenants moved out. The house was a duplex, but there were no children in either family. Therefore, we did not think it should take either family long to find another house. We hoped it would not be more than ninety days. In fact, we hoped it would be much less, and that a lot of the money we had been paying for rent might go into repairs. We hoped we would be able to move in by Christmas (we made the down payment in October) or at least by our first birthday, the feast of the Epiphany.

Our family had grown. Therese had been born shortly after Dorothy left, on the feast of SS. Simon and Jude. Denise was very proud of her new daughter, and already Bubble and Roy loved their new little sister. We managed to squeeze one of the tiny white cribs we had received from St. Peter's orphanage into the room with Denise for the baby. Every day, until the baby was baptized at two weeks of age, Father Robert came up the block from the church to the house to bring Our Lord to Denise, except two days when he could not. Blessed Martin House seemed to me to take on a new splendor, a sort of grandeur, in all its poverty and ugliness, because of this Guest who came there.

Two new mothers arrived also, close upon one another. There was Myrtle with her infant daughter and five-year-old son, who needed temporary shelter, and Frances and her two-year (almost) son. She was expecting another baby and was sick in her mind as well. Both worked, Myrtle for twelve dollars a week, and Frances doing day work whenever she could find it.

Somewhere around the big room we managed to find

beds for all to sleep in. Hence the nights were not so bad—except when the babies cried for long stretches. But the lack of privacy, of a place where one could think, could rest, could be at peace with oneself, drove the women wild in the daytime, especially Frances, already so unstable and needing but a push to throw her completely out of balance.

Most of the bickering was over the children. None of the three wanted either of the others to try to discipline her children; yet, except for Frances, all wanted to discipline the others' children. Sometimes, when I had gone over to my mother's house on Sunday, I would have to come back to the house to settle a quarrel which threatened to become a fight, between two of them, or all of the three.

I knew most of it was due to our crowded condition, the poverty and fear of the women who worried about tomorrow and projected their worries onto the visible people around them—and due to the lack of privacy. Part of it came from feelings of insecurity and a lack of a sense of being loved. The last thing would take much time; the other things could not be helped until we moved. Mother, Ida, and I tried to keep peace among the women and prayed for the new house, that we would soon really have it.

Meanwhile Christmas was coming. In the Outer Circle, we planned things for the children, and in the nursery and what was left of the Community Center, we planned things for the Outer Circle and for the other people who had been kind and generous to the children during the year.

The children helped me to build a crib out of an old wooden box and painted it. We bought some statues and carved others from soap. We decorated the room with paper and tinsel and had a tiny Infant Jesus lying in straw on the table.

We practiced a little play, based on the Christmas story. The school children, like Mary Lou and Mary Lee, sang carols behind a curtain, while the pre-school children acted. The four- and five-year-olds had speaking parts. There were St. Elizabeth, St. Joseph, the Blessed Virgin, the Inn Keeper, shepherds, Wise Men, and angels. The two- and three-year-olds were lambs and sheep, all covered with cotton for wool. An infant was the Holy Child. All the costumes were simple; long dresses for the robes, tablecloths and scarves for the hoods and turbans, enriched by satin ribbon for the Wise Men. Butch, who was St. Joseph, wore my nurse's cape and carried a staff in his hand.

In the first scene, the Blessed Virgin knelt praying and an angel came. The six-year-old announcer said, "Once there was a Virgin and the Virgin's name was Mary. Then an angel came."

The curtain was drawn back to show the kneeling figure of the Blessed Virgin.

An angel, dressed in white curtains, came on stage.

"Hail, Mary, full of grace," he greeted her. "You are going to have a little baby named Jesus."

The virgin was troubled. "How can that be?" she asked.

"God will do it," the angel promised, and went away.

In the next scene, the Virgin went to see her cousin. "Blessed art thou among women," she said, and they embraced.

The curtain closed again and the children sang, "O Come, O Come, Emmanuel." When it opened again, St.

Joseph lay on the floor tossing restlessly. "I'm so worried about Mary," he kept repeating. "I'm so worried about Mary."

An angel came. "Joseph, don't be afraid to take Mary for your wife. Mary is going to be the Mother of God."

Again the scene changed, while the children sang, "O Little Town of Bethlehem."

Mary and Joseph were looking for a place to stay. St. Joseph said to Mary, "Don't worry, Mary. I'll find some place for us to stay."

He went up to the Inn Keeper. "We are tired and we have no place to go. Can we stay here with you?"

The Inn Keeper shook his head. "We don't have any room," he told him, "but you can sleep in the stable."

Once more the scene changed. The shepherds were watching their sheep. The little lambs kept wandering offstage, to the consternation of the shepherds and the amusement of the audience.

Three angels came and sang "Glory, Glory, Glory," and the big children sang, "Angels We Have Heard on High."

In the last scene a real little infant lay in the straw playing, while the rest of the little Holy Family looked on. Angels came to sing and kneel in adoration. The shepherds brought the little sheep, and Wise Men came bringing gifts. When all were in their places, the little ones sang "Silent Night" and the curtain was drawn for the last time.

The children loved acting their parts, especially dressed up. It took no persuasion at all to get them to present the short play for each group that came to bring them gifts. The groups who came seemed to enjoy it equally. They had come in joy, to bring joy to these little ones in Christ, expecting nothing in return and wanting nothing in return. Because of that, they were given something of great value in return, the gratitude of children and a share in their spirit of joy.

All the children and the parents received many gifts, things they needed, like food, and things they wanted, like toys and candy. The children who lived in the house, and several others, received tricycles. The others received smaller gifts, but all were delighted.

Christmas Eve Denise and I, and five of the girls from the Community Center, took candles and went out caroling on the streets. People seemed very surprised to see us but glad, too. Some invited us into their homes to find warmth and gave us candy, fruit, and nuts. Some sang with us, while we were before their homes.

We sang until eleven o'clock, ending at my mother's house. We then went to church at St. Bridget's, all of us, including Mother. We were early, so we listened to the children there singing as the church filled up.

It was easy to believe the Christ was born that night. Had we not seen Him ourselves being reborn in the hearts of the lonely and the discouraged at Blessed Martin House, who had come for help and found love? Had we not seen Him in the hearts of white people who had come there despising, or looking down upon, colored people, as they learned to love us? Had we not seen Him being born in the hearts of Negroes who had come hating white people, suspicious of them, fearful and distrustful of them, as they learned to love and trust? Had we not seen Him being born over and over in the stable of human suffering because there was no room for Him in the Inn of human hearts?

"The Word was made flesh!" The Word had become

flesh all around us in a different manner. Christ became man that we might become other Christs, that we might become a part of Him and of each other. "That they all may be one as Thou, Father, in me and I in Thee; that they also may be one in Us." Blessed Martin House was another stable where Christ came in the persons of the poor and unloved because there was no room for them anywhere else. And the Wise Men had brought Him gifts, gold, in the money and other material things our friends had brought; frankincense, in the prayers they had said for us and the joys they had given us, seeing our dignity as God's own beneath the shabbiness and ugliness of poverty; and myrrh, in the suffering that was a part of it too, because some people could not see or understand.

After Mass there was a party for the children. We sang songs and had turkey and cake and candy, nuts and fruit. We opened presents and rejoiced with each other.

At last, tired, but very happy, we all went to bed, after seeing the children safely home who could not stay all night with us.

There was so much work to be done, and so little time to rest, that by New Year's day I had used up all my reserve energy, and the feast of the Circumcision found me with a mild case of flu. My doctor didn't like my cough and told me to rest more. So I went down the block to Mass every morning and came home to rest most of the day in bed, while Denise and Myrtle took care of the house and children with Ida.

January sixth, the feast of the Epiphany, was our first birthday. When it arrived, it found us very aware of the great things God had done in us and for us and through us during the year. And it was in a spirit of deep gratitude that we offered together with Father Murphy, a Solemn High Mass of Thanksgiving at St. Bridget's Church. Our friends Father Robert and Father Hostettler were the deacon and subdeacon. Two seminarians served the Mass, and Denise and I, the children who sang with us at St. Bridget's, and members of the Outer Circle and Volunteers sang the Mass.

Afterwards there was a communion breakfast at St. Bridget's, and we talked about the house, about some of the things that had happened during the past year. We talked about the serious things—like the time a woman had gone off and left her baby for days and refused to come get him. Finally I had had to take him to her at her work. We talked about the sorrowful things, like Frances' mental condition and the confusion it was causing in the house. We talked about the funny things, like Bob's diapering efforts and the time we had taken the children fishing and run out of water before Morris came back for us, so that I had had to hitch-hike a ride to West Memphis, Arkansas, to get us something to drink.

After breakfast I went home and went back to bed to rest. Mother, Ida, Denise, and the volunteers cleaned up. I thought I would be better by the next day, but I was worse and had to remain in bed for the next two weeks, except for visits to the doctor. For the first time, I really felt like a Cusan, and I was glad I had something real to suffer, that I could see and understand. It was good to have time to really pray, too. During rest hours and the other rare peaceful moments, I could lose myself in God. I had no need to think or worry about anything else. And best of all was the daily visit of our parish priest, who brought Our Lord to me. Again and again

I thanked God for placing us in this parish with this priest.

I needed the grace of the Sacrament too, because there was no peace in the house. My bed was separated from the nursery only by a thin curtain, and the children ran in and out all day. I helped to feed and diaper them when the others were busy about other things. The table where the children, and all of us, ate, was in the same little alcove, so I had company at every mealtime. Worst of all was the constant quarrelling and bickering among the women in the house, which still continued. Since Denise had lived there longest and knew the way things were usually done at Blessed Martin House best, she took the greatest responsibility for the house. She was effectively in charge while I was ill. The others resented that, partly through envy and partly for some reason more obscure, which I could sense but not define.

Frances' mental condition grew worse under the pressure, for she needed sympathy, understanding, security— and above all, patience and love. Yet neither Denise nor Myrtle was prepared to give her these things. Trifles rose like mountains and caused endless unrest.

Frances began imagining that even the mothers who came to bring their children to the nursery were "thrilling over her" (her expression) and stealing her personality. Her thoughts and expressions were so confused and disjointed, so disturbed and distorted, it was hard to understand what she meant by them, or even to be sure whether her words had any meaning at all. Nevertheless she loved her baby, and the one on the way, and worked every day she could to help herself and them. She carried the big two-year-old around like a tiny infant with an unnatural possessiveness. Even in this, you could see her sickness, because there was an unnatural sensuality in the way she touched him and kissed him.

I gave myself leave to get out of bed one day when conditions became very bad, and went down to the Court-house and to Juvenile Court to see if she could be hospitalized. There I learned that she had already been held in jail once as mentally defective after she had threatened to kill someone. However, since she was not a resident of the state, but had come from Detroit, she was not eligible for hospitalization in Memphis. She could not even see a doctor in the clinic unless the maternity clinic recommended her for psychopathic examination. There was nothing anyone could do, various officials told me, unless she became violent, in which case I could call the police.

At last, in one office, a man told me that her father, who was a resident, could come and swear out a lunacy warrant, in which case she would be arrested and held until they were able to send her back to Detroit.

Actually, I believed that as a Negro patient she would receive much better care in Detroit than in Tennessee, because our state sanatorium has an unenviable reputation, even for white patients. So I was a little glad she couldn't go out to Bolivar, though that left the problem still at Blessed Martin's door, and Frances still on our hands.

Father Murphy and I talked to her father and at last persuaded him to swear out the warrant. Finally, after a particularly violent (in words) episode, she was taken into custody and the baby was left at the house with me. He was a good little fellow, but he missed her very much and sometimes looked for her. I tried to be mother to him and give him the love and affection he needed. Gradually he stopped watching for her and began to trust me.

Another month passed. The people moved from one

side of the new house and we began our repairs. We found a reasonable plumber, and carpenter, who started to work, adding a new room for a bathroom.

Denise asked me one day what she would have to do to become a part of the house. Over the months, she had shown more and more interest in the work, so I had expected the question and was prepared for it. There were still many things she did not understand, but she was willing to try to learn them and had already grown so much in grace that I thought she should try, if she willed, this way of life.

"You would have to take more responsibility, more initiative. You would have to try and love the mothers and the children, with a love that asks no return, loving Christ in them, for His sake. You would have to try to be more patient and try to be much less ready to take offense."

"I'd like to try it. I've been thinking a lot about it. But the thing that has held me back is the thought of my children. I have three now, what would happen to them?"

"That is something to think about, all right. But consider this too—how much more can you offer them otherwise? You are not trained for anything. With wages what they are for colored women, you will be fortunate if you can barely support them alone anyway, unless you can get A.D.C. or some other aid for children. Isn't that true?"

"That's right," she admitted.

"Here they would be like Butch, dependent on the house for food and ordinary needs, wearing the clothes that are given to us, as we do. And like Butch, they could share in any money I make personally, by writing or otherwise, for any extraordinary needs. If you did come into the work wholeheartedly, you would be a tremendous help, and the house could do more. There should be more than just myself, there should be a community. We could have community prayer and activities which are impossible to me alone. Of course, I would be glad to have you. But I warn you. It is not easy. It takes a lot of giving—of yourself—and a lot of love. Peter Maurin said, 'People used to say about the Christians: See how they love each other. Now they say: See how they pass the buck.' We want to restore the proper order."

"I want to try," Denise offered.

"It's okay with me. If it doesn't work out, you won't lose anything, and will have gained a lot spiritually. But pray over it."

"I will," she promised, and did.

After a few days or a week, we talked about it again. "I've decided to try it," she said resolutely.

So Denise became a part of the house, a fellow worker. And I was no longer alone.

21

As the work of repairing the new house grew, I was very glad that Denise had decided to stay at the house. We planned to build on an extra room, because she would need a room for herself and her children if she decided to stay permanently. On the other hand, if, at some later date, she changed her mind, I hoped other staff workers would come. Then they would need the room. We wanted to have one room for Outer Circle meetings and as a "nice" room to receive visitors. This would be the lounge of the teen-agers, too, if they started coming again. We wanted a room for the nursery, one to be used as combined dining-room and playroom, and a dormitory for women. The two small end rooms we planned to use, one as kitchen, and one for Butch and me.

While the carpenter worked on the new rooms, Denise and I, the mothers of the children in the nursery, and some girls from Sienna began tearing the dirty, torn wallpaper from the walls. There were layers and layers of it. Often huge chunks of plaster came down with it and we knocked off that around it which was loose.

We washed the walls and a boy from C.B.C. came down to help us paint.

One day in the middle of it all, Myrtle came and got her children and clothes without saying anything to anyone. We were surprised but also a little glad, because she had begun staying out late at night instead of coming home to her children when she left her job in the evening. We never saw her any more, so we never learned what happened to her.

In a few days Jackie had moved in with us. She, too, was expecting a child and had no one in Memphis who cared about her. She was very young, only eighteen, and a lovely girl. She pitched right in and helped with the work. When Denise and I started painting inside the new house, she was there helping. Even the children helped. Butch, Lawrence, and Nathaniel, Ruby's son, painted the bathroom walls, while I did the ceiling. The children in the nursery, from three years up, put on old clothing and painted all the tables and chairs and baby beds. We adults went over them only to finish spots they missed, or smooth rough or uneven places. The children were very proud of themselves and bragged to their mothers about their accomplishments.

The mothers helped, too. They kept Blessed Martin House open, cared for the children, and sometimes cooked supper while we painted. Some came over to the new house and helped with the painting.

I learned to plaster small holes with cement and to mix the cement. I filled in a lot of the small holes, leaving the big ones for a man experienced in that trade.

About that time, a group of students from C.B.C. became interested in the project and came down more and more often to help with the work. We were nearly finished with the painting on the inside, but there were some ceilings yet to be done. They finished these for us. Then they cut and laid the linoleum on all the floors, fixing one of them badly in need of repairs. We began painting outside while the plumbers finished up their job inside.

We weren't finished with the outside painting before our rent came due. We decided to move instead of paying another month's advance. The boys from C.B.C. and Morris helped us. Only three rooms were ready, so we moved into these. We still had no water nor gas, so we used electric heaters and an oil heater which smoked so much at times that the whole room would suddenly be filled with a black dense cloud of soot which covered everything. We cooked on a little portable oil stove with only one burner and an oven that could be removed at will.

It was March, and still very cold. The electric heaters warmed only a few feet. We had to heat water for washing, cleaning, and bathing. And we had to cook meals for six people all on the one burner—besides warming the children's lunches and milk.

We had acquired a new puppy which wasn't yet housebroken, and she kept us mopping. We were glad that the cats were very clean, so we didn't have to clean after them, too. We wished Theresa, the puppy, was a little more like them.

Every day Denise kept the house and children with the help of the mothers, and the students from C.B.C., and I painted and fixed the yard and garden. Sometimes Denise helped me too, or one of the mothers. Mr. Huddleston, our carpenter, who had become also our friend, gave us a lot of suggestions about paint and building and other things, which saved us many dollars.

Morris carried us into the country to get grass seeds and manure for the yard. We put all of this out, hoping we could get something to grow from the sickly-looking soil. We planted corn, beans, cabbage, tomatoes, peanuts, and squash in the garden and added fertilizer in the same hope.

The students from C.B.C. entered not only into the work of the house, but also into its spirit. They organized a group at school called "Helpers of the House of Hospitality." They began putting out a little mimeographed sheet for each other, called "Impact." They chose that name because it was the impact of the Church's doctrine of the Mystical Body of Christ which awakened their interest in the house and sense of responsibility towards it. It was this doctrine that had set them to thinking of the problems of the Negro people in their midst, and made them want to do something about it. They came with such open and genuine humility and charity, that all at the house loved them and thought of them as friends. They shamed prejudice out of others, who might otherwise have been awed by or resentful of the white skins God gave them.

Besides this, we had discussions about the house and the spirit of the work. We talked informally about the doctrine of the Mystical Body as we wanted to apply it here, seeing Christ in each other, and in those who came to us in His name. We talked about poverty, and they were not scandalized at our way of life, at our utter dependence upon the Providence of God for all our needs. They invited me to speak at the school (and later, when we were settled, I did), and talk about the work.

Moreover, they loved the children, and were loved by them. Whenever they came, Butch, Bubble, and some of the others were ready for a good romp and roughhouse, and the boys obliged, laughingly. One said, "They remind me of my little brothers," in a voice tender and a little amazed.

They talked to me about their families, and it was good to see their conscience grow to include care for other families of a different race from their own in their regard. It was good to see them coming to an understanding of the human needs of people, of the problems and suffering of human beings like themselves with different colored skins but with the same joys and ambitions. It was like witnessing a new birth sometimes, inspiring in the beholder not only joy, but a sense of awe and reverence for the power of God and His Goodness.

The little sheet "Impact" expressed so well their growth and spirit that we borrowed from it for our monthly newsletter for *Volunteers' News*.

On the feast of St. Joseph, they wrote:

> In the Litany of St. Joseph, however, there is one title under which we invoke him that seems to fit very well for House of Hospitality Helpers. Joseph is the Model of Artisans—the model for workers.
>
> And surely those of the Helpers who have gone down to the House know it is a matter of *work*. So it would be well for each man in the group to ponder well today the aspects of St. Joseph's life which reveal for us the thinking that should go into our work at the house. Joseph, the diligent, we might add to the great litany of titles that he already has—Joseph, the strong, Joseph, the persevering, even when the going is rough—Joseph, the careful, especially when the work is that of painstaking labor—Joseph

the patient, especially with a job that is difficult and long being done—Joseph, the humble, in a job that seems so very menial, so low, so humbling! Surely you can find the litany applied to you in your work at the House of Hospitality. Go to Joseph, then, and pray that in your work for Christ, *which was his life in total,* you may imitate him, the Spouse of the Most Blessed Mother, the Guardian of the Child Jesus, the MODEL OF ARTISANS.

Moreover, they wrote funny stories about the children. Bill Wym wrote:

Tex Rides Again

During my first visit to the "House," I was helping to lay linoleum when three small colored streaks sped past us, heading for the adjoining room. After a few minutes, the sound of bullets ceased and a cry for help, mixed with laughter, emerged from the same room.

Getting up, I peered into the "wide open country" and saw that one of the cowboys, presumably the Villain, had caught himself in the window. He had been attempting an escape, which resulted in the window closing on his back. After being rescued, "Tex" thanked me and rode off into the sunset.

Some of the members of the Outer Circle, like Linda, Alice, and Eugenia helped in various ways too, and tried to get others to help. Alice, of course, had been one spirit with the house since our visit to the Bishop together, and Eugenia had seemed to understand much of the spirit for a long time, ever since the house had first opened. But with Linda it was different. Our friendship and her understanding had grown together, and I had seen in her changes of attitude toward my people and the work, which made me very glad, even while it humbled me. Alice was always a friend. Linda became a friend. Alice had seemed to have no prejudice to conquer. Linda had done a heroic job of conquering it in herself.

In the middle of our work of repairing, Betty Schneider, the national Director of Friendship House, came up to Memphis from a visit to New Orleans and spoke to the group of students from C.B.C., Sienna and some other volunteers and members of the Outer Circle. She talked about Friendship House and its interracial apostolate.

The talk served to encourage the students and the white volunteers very much in their interest in and work for the house. It was good for them to see that other white people like themselves were interested in this problem, that some were giving their lives to God in a special way to do something about it. They too must have felt lonely at times, being of the very few who thought and believed a certain way. Some I knew were the only ones in their families who thought in a Christian way about race and the problems of poverty of the Negro.

I know how much it means to have someone like you believe as you believe and live according to the principles by which you are trying to live. I know also how lonely is that loneliness that comes from being different in thought or action or belief from the people around you, the people you love, the people with whom you must live, even though your way be right, even though it be God's way for you.

Of course, He gives you something greater than your loneliness, that more than makes up for it. He gives you little by little, as you can bear it, and as you give yourself, a share in His own life, which has in it all fullness and joy. And even when the fullness and joy are obscure and remote from the senses, some consciousness remains of it, so you know you would not exchange this Thing He has given you, with all its suffering, for anything the mind can conceive or the heart can desire. For to have God is to have everything, and to have all else besides, without Him, is to have nothing. He fills you, even while you are conscious of your emptiness, and is with you even when you are most alone—perhaps especially then; that is the paradox of Christianity.

Betty Schneider only stayed a few hours, but she accomplished much in them, in all of us, in those few hours. She went with us to see the new house. She could see its possibilities and liked it. We invited her to come again and visit longer when the house was finished.

"I may," she promised. "In fact, you may be seeing a lot of us soon. There is the possibility that we will open a house down in Shreveport."

That was good news. That meant we would be neighbors. "When?" I wanted to know.

She could not give a definite date then. It would have to be decided by the council of all the houses of Friendship House.

"Probably very soon." She could not be more definite than that.

After she had gone, the repairs continued for about three weeks or more beyond the time we actually moved into the new house. At last, however, one day we were finished.

Dick Neville, one of the students from C.B.C., looked on the house with pride, as it stood there, shining white and blue in the sunshine, from the coats of paint he had helped to apply. He looked across the way at its twin, still for sale by the same people from whom we had bought this one. It looked like one of the before-and-after advertisements some magazines like to carry.

"We ought to buy the other one, too," he told me, "just to fix it up."

I laughed. "Sure, any day now. All we need is a couple of thousand dollars more for repairs and down payment. You got it?"

He laughed too. "Not today," he admitted. "But the boys have been talking about it. I wish we could."

"I wish you could, too," I told him. "Some day, we're going to have another house, just for the women who need shelter and friendship and understanding and an example of Christian living to show them it is possible to live so and be happy. We're going to have a farm, too, and a retreat house where we can go and others can come to learn to know and love God better. It will be interracial, like the house, so anyone can come, men and women, colored and white, it won't matter. God will be there, Head of the House. In the summer, the children can go there for camping or picnics. We can grow our own food and can it. And the farm can be a house of hospitality on the land. Some of the women and children can stay there more or less permanently, helping us while we help them."

"We hope so," Dick agreed. "We are certainly praying for the project."

After the students had gone that week, Denise and I cleaned the house and put fresh spreads on the bed and scarves around on tables and chests. The next day was Good Friday, and Alice had promised to keep Butch while

I made the Three Hours at St. Peter's. I planned to be away all day, so wanted everything ready for the morrow.

The house seemed to us beautiful with its bright new colors, green and yellow, rose and blue, aquamarine and red, all bright colors to delight the eyes of children. In the parlor, the big statue of Blessed Martin de Porres seemed to laugh down at the vase of flowers before it, and from the wall, our Black Madonna smiled. The piano, which a friend had given, gleamed softly in the sunlight, and the new couch covers seemed to reflect its brightness. We liked the new house.

On Holy Saturday Father Murphy had promised to come and bless the house. We had hoped Bishop Adrian would come, and invited him to do so, but he had answered that it would be some time before he came to Memphis again. He had suggested that Father Murphy bless it instead, on Holy Saturday.

Holy Saturday dawned a beautiful day. I went to St. Bridget's early and sang the Mass and the Litany of the Saints with the children. I returned and had breakfast, and not long after, Father Murphy came and brought Mr. Childs. We sang the Litany of the Saints again, and Father blessed the house and those who lived therein and the garden and the yard. He even blessed Tom Cat, and St. Theresa of Avila, our silly little puppy who insisted on running under our feet.

Afterwards we talked together a long time with a deep contentment. He said this was one of those days he would always remember. I agreed. It had been bought at great cost, but it was the pearl of great price which the man sold all his goods to possess. I would remember it too.

That afternoon we had an egg hunt for the neighborhood children and gave out toys and candy to those who found the least. We also gave each mother a nice bunny or doll for her children out of a big box of new toys which had come in for Easter.

Easter Sunday was a day between God and me. There was that which it does not seem to me can be shared or expressed. I was completely happy and at peace. Butch went with me to church, and later that evening I carried him somewhere else. I don't remember where. It doesn't matter. God was there. He was everywhere, filling me so completely that there was no room for anything else, no matter what was being done or said. No room, no need. He was All, in all, through all.

22

THE MONTHS PASSED SWIFTLY IN THE NEW HOUSE. IN THE spring, Denise went to Grailville to learn more about the lay apostolate, and I kept her children for her.

While she was gone the work kept growing. Jackie left and two more young girls came to live at the house, one expecting a baby, the other already with a six-months-old child. There were about fifteen children in the nursery as well, most days.

In the summer I kept my promise to return to Caritas. I went down to teach the children in the day camp music, and to learn something myself about crafts, for the benefit of my own children at Blessed Martin House. Butch and Denise's children went down with me, and Butch and Bubble took part in the activities of the day camp. Mrs. Becton kept Denise's baby while we were away.

At Caritas I did learn a lot about a day camp and a little about crafts, but the most important things I learned were not the ones I had come there to learn—I learned more about children. Both Mary Linda and Bertha had taught, and were teaching, children, and their knowledge and experience took for granted what I did not even know.

There was much about planning programs and activities that seem so simple but which were really the result of much time and thought. Their ideas on discipline were new to me too, and I could not believe in them for a long time (not, in fact, until I returned home and tried to put some of them into effect myself). I found them more difficult because they called for more self-discipline, but for most children beyond the toddling stage, they now seem to me better. Their idea was to keep the children busy with planned projects and to limit corporal punishment almost to the point of non-existence; teach the child, also, to act according to reason; give the motive of love.

When I returned to the house, I tried to be more consistent in planning activities for the children, and more scrupulous. With so little help and so many other activities besides the children's nursery, there never could be programs comparable to those of the day camp, but there certainly was a marked improvement in the nursery routine and in the children's attitudes after I tried to put into effect some of the things I had learned at Caritas. There was the same battle with some of the mothers on their days to help with the work at the house, because they did not want to play with the children, or to try to teach them, but were content to let them make their own games and play with a minimum of supervision. But I found that it was when these mothers were in charge that the couch covers were torn, the walls were written over, the toys were broken up. This alone spoke well for the Caritas way.

After I came back from Caritas, I was in Memphis at the house for about a month, until Denise came back; then I went to New York to make a retreat again, and to talk to Mrs. Brunner about writing a book about C.U.S.A. Father Casey from Minnesota gave the retreat this time, and I found it even more helpful than before. I was very troubled about prayer, and it seemed to me that I could no longer pray, but Father Casey reassured me and helped me to find peace in this regard.

I was not able to see Mrs. Brunner because she was still in Europe, but with her secretary I made tentative plans. I would be able to talk to her later, on her return, if I could come back to New York.

While I was away, I had to go to Peabody, Massachusetts, too, to get Butch, who had spent the part of the summer since we had returned from New Orleans there with friends. In a quiet, unobtrusive way, these friends also wanted to help in the interracial apostolate. So quietly, and without fuss or fanfare, they had taken a little colored boy into their home, as one of the family, for some six weeks.

When he first came, they said, a few in the all-white neighborhood seemed to resent him, and they would not permit their children to play with him. But in a very short time he had won them over, and at the time he left all the children were playing with him and he had many friends.

Shortly after I came back, Denise decided that the work of the lay apostolate was not her vocation. She had given it more than a year's trial, but Blessed Martin House was just not for her. For awhile she considered marrying a nice young man who had been coming to see her; but in the end, she decided to get a job and work for a time on her own.

When I returned, there was a new pastor at St. Bridget's. He had come before I went away, but I had never met him. Now I did.

There was never another priest like Father Gray.

There couldn't have been! The man who wrote *The Little World of Don Camillo* may have met his shadow, for Father Gray reminds me much of Don Camillo. But he's in a class by himself.

He must be about sixty, more or less; he is of medium height, and round of face and body. He wears a funny little goatee and talks with an accent that would make a most powerful secret weapon if ever aural warfare were used. Even Brooklyn never sounded like that. When he offers a low Mass, not even the server can follow him. When he offers a high Mass, he sings most of it off-key, or in a monotone, but every once in awhile, and always at the *Pater Noster*, he takes a deep breath and gives out a loud, strong tone, clear as a bell, à la Caruso.

All during the Mass he talks to the servers, so every Mass is for them a class in rubrics, and if we do or sing something wrong in the choir, he doesn't hesitate to turn and tell us about it, either. "Stop that laughing up there!" he told the children one day. And on another occasion, when we started to sing a hymn after Mass: "Some day I'm going to teach you something about rubrics." Once at the Preface, when the altar boys forgot to stand, he sang out, in a clear chant: "Stand! Stand!"

Yet, with all his eccentricities, there is no irreverence in his Mass. On the contrary, it is as if he and Our Lord have grown so close, and are such familiar friends, that he can dare what others would not.

I wondered how he would treat us, from Blessed Martin House, what he would think of the house. Denise and I continued to sing the Masses with the girls from the parish, and one day, when there was no server, offered to give the responses. He made no objection to either practice, but instead, after that, seemed to expect us to sing alone when the girls were not there (as we had always done), and to give the responses with the server even when the server was there. One day, I remember, we started not to do this, when we saw that the altar boy had come, but Father Gray turned and gave us such a look that we have been answering ever since.

After he knew us better he would call us to fix the flowers on the altar or to light the candles and set up the altar for Mass and put away the things afterward. He would call me to put away the vestments and Denise to turn out the lights. "We'll have to make you temporary sacristan," he told me one day.

I liked to do these things, and so did Denise. They made us feel very close to Our Lord and very much a part of His church. However, occasionally I would be in a bit of a hurry and hope he would not call me. He would be sure to call me then. "Come on, Helen, put away these things," he would say. "That is more meritorious than your private prayer." I would obey, but once I tried to point out that mental prayer was important too. He laughed at me. "Hush, child, you worry yourself too much. Father Joe says the same thing. If you don't watch out, you are going to have a nervous breakdown, just like he said. St. Benedict says to work is to pray. You don't have to spend a half-hour in meditation. When you come to Mass, and say your morning and night prayers, that is enough. Your good work at the house is prayer enough."

So you've been talking to Father Joe about me, I thought, Oh, oh. Aloud I said, "Father, the only time I can rest in the day is when I pray. Once I leave here in the morning—that's it."

"Uh, huh." He shook his head. "You could pray just as well at home."

"You don't know my house, Father. Did you ever try to meditate with seventeen children around?"

He admitted he had not.

"Try it some time," I invited him.

"Go for a long walk, then. You try and think too much. Don't get mad at me, now. I'm just telling you for your own good."

"I'm not mad, Father, I know you are. But I really don't worry. I rest when I pray. Father Joe doesn't know me very well, so you can't always believe him entirely. He doesn't understand about the house or any part of the lay apostolate."

"I'm not going by what he says. I'm just telling you. I really don't know him that well."

"All right, Father."

And I never got angry. You can't get angry with Father Gray, no matter what he says. There is just something about the way he says even the hardest things that makes anger out of the question. Your own conscience makes excuses for him—"His arthritis must be bothering him a lot today." And quite possibly that is right, for he is not a well man. Often at Mass he cannot kneel, and you can see that even walking costs pain and effort. But he bears the pain and puts out the effort.

"Pray that I will be able to walk tomorrow," he will say, "so I can say Mass. Whenever the weather changes, I have a hard time." And we promise.

One day we were talking again and he said to me: "You want to have your own way too much. You won't listen to your pastor, Father Joe, or obey him . . ."

"Father Joe is not my pastor, Father, you are my pastor," I told him.

"Uh, uh." He shook his head. "You belong to the colored parish."

"Oh, no, Father. Canon Law says I have the right to belong to the parish in which I live. I live in your parish."

"No, but all the colored people belong to one of the two colored parishes."

"Canon Law, Father . . . "

"Are you going to tell me something about Canon Law? I am a theologian. Canon Law doesn't say that. The Church also has to obey civil law, you know."

"That may be so, Father, as long as civil law is not against the law of God. But anyway, there is no civil law that says colored and white cannot belong to the same church. It is bad enough that they should make a law like that for schools—and many say even this is unconstitutional for public schools—but no state has dared to make a law regarding churches. That is one of the fundamental rights guaranteed by the Constitution, freedom of religion. That excuse won't hold up, Father. If it would, do you think that Archbishop Rummel could have gotten away with what he did in New Orleans or Bishop Waters in North Carolina? These people were just as prejudiced as the Catholics in Memphis, but those bishops spoke for the Church."

"But they didn't say that."

"They all said, and the Holy Father says,* that we all have equal rights in the house of God! You see, you are

---

* "Those who enter the Church, whatever be their origin or their speech, must know that they have equal rights as children in the House of the Lord, where the Law of Christ and the peace of Christ prevail."

—*Summi Pontificatus*

my pastor. You may disown me, if you like, as many white fathers disown their colored children. But you are, for all of that."

"Do you know that if you were dying, I could not even bring you the last Sacraments?"

"You could if you wanted to. In conscience, I think you would be bound to, if I called you. I could not make you, of course. But really not only the colored Catholics in your parish, but all the baptized people in your parish, even the non-Catholics, belong to your parish. In a certain sense, you are responsible for their souls too."

"Hush, child," he said. "You don't know what you are talking about. Go on, now, tell the boy to light three candles."

"All right, Father."

"And don't get mad at me."

"I'm not mad at you, Father. How can I be mad at my pastor?" I said, laughingly, as I went out the door.

"And don't sing a hymn, either, at the Offertory."

"I won't, The only reason we have been doing it is that that is the way sister taught the children. I try not to change anything without good reason and without knowing it's okay."

"The sisters can be wrong too. I'm holding you responsible."

"Okay," I agreed, and went on to do his bidding.

I was telling Mother about it later, though, and I said to her, "If I die while you are alive, I want to be buried from St. Bridget's parish, as I have lived in St. Bridget's parish. I believe in one, holy, Catholic Church. If there is another, a colored Catholic Church, I know nothing of it. The Pope speaks of the heresy of race, so if any Church teaches that one race is inferior to another, and insists that

253

that inferior race must belong to a different church from other races, then that Church is teaching heresy, and a religion of men, not of God. But if I must die according to a religion made up, or formed, according to the prejudices of men, then I would die according to a religion of my own people. I will live for my faith, and, if God will, die for it; but if I must die for any other, I want it to be some nice African Methodist something-or-other. Bury me in Clayborne Temple, if you want to." (That was an African Methodist church near by.)

Mother just laughed at me. "I'll send you to New York and bury you," she said.

Afterwards I was ashamed of my outburst. I could see that once again I was setting a limit to what I was willing to give God, when He has said we must love Him without limit. I was saying, "I will bear this cross but not that one." I wanted to suffer for Our Lord in my own way instead of His. "I'm sorry," I told Him. "I will try to do better. Help me to do better." I wondered if I would ever learn patience.

A day or so later, I was in the sacristy again and Father Gray asked me. "How is your little boy?"

Butch had received a blow on his eye the previous week and was in the hospital. We did not know yet whether he would regain his sight in the eye.

"I don't know, Father. He feels much better now, but we just don't know about the eye. You say a prayer for him."

"I'll do that. But why don't you pray to Saint Lucy? She is the patron for that need."

"All right, I will."

"You told everybody else about him, but you didn't tell me."

"Yes, I did, Father. You forgot. I told you he was in the hospital the other day when we were talking. I just told the others because they were going to take me to the hospital to visit him."

"I'd go visit him."

"Would you really? You still can. He would love to have you, I know. And I would love to have you go."

"All right. I'll go Monday, or maybe tomorrow if I have the time. I can't go today."

"Monday is fine. Try and go then."

So he promised. That was Father Gray for you, wholly unpredictable. I guess that is one reason we found it easy to love him.

The next week the surgeons at the hospital operated on Butch's eye. I was not notified and knew nothing about it until I came to the hospital that evening. It was the city hospital, and when he had been admitted, I had signed what the admission office had assured me was an "emergency consent" for operation, which would only be used if an emergency operation became necessary. But that had been a whole week before, and this could no longer be considered an emergency. I was furious.

And to make matters worse, one of the white nurses told me that I could not visit him until visiting day, three days away, when I could come and look at him through a glass window. I could not talk to him nor he to me, because you could not hear through the glass.

"Why was I not notified about the operation?" I demanded.

"We could not reach you," she said. "We called over to Isolation, but you weren't there."

"It has been two years since I worked in Isolation. I left a number here."

She did not say anything, but walked away.

I went down to hall to see Butch, despite her objection.

Once more my mind was a turmoil of chaotic thought and rebellion. Why must the poor be defenseless, and why must the Negro be the poorest of the poor? Already I had forgotten the lesson of a few days past, and my good resolution. I hushed the voice of God within me and refused to listen to it. I let myself be filled with the darkness and coldness. I wallowed in the mud of my own misery like a pig, and stifled in myself the impulse to come up into the clean air of God's presence.

For two days I was like that. I went to Mass and Communion, but there was no heart in it. I went because in my darkness, God gave me deep down inside me where I could not understand it nor explain it, light enough to see the need I had of His presence, even though I could take no comfort in it.

But Our God is infinitely patient and loving and merciful, and gently He wooed my silly soul and warmed my coldness and lightened my darkness, until one day, kneeling before Him in the Tabernacle, before Mass, I knew how foolish I was and how wrong. "I am a jealous God," He says, "thou shalt have no other gods before me."

No other gods. Not even myself. Not my son. Not my race. Just Him.

"Everyone of you that does not renounce all that he possesses can not be My disciple," he said. Yet how many things I wanted to hold just for myself. "Take up your cross," He said. But as always, I wanted a cross only of my own choosing. I was willing to suffer only if I could choose the way I would suffer.

But it wouldn't do. We must die to live, dying first to what is ours, then to ourselves. At last I found in my-

256

self the grace to make the act of will He wanted of me: "Behold the servant of the Lord, be it done unto me according to Thy word," I repeated Our Lady's *Fiat;* then Our Lord's: "Thy will, not mine."

That night when I went back to the hospital, Butch was feeling fine. His eye was still bandaged, of course, but he didn't have a headache any more. A specialist I had called at the suggestion of a friend, who offered to pay for it, had come to look at him. He told me that the operation seemed to have been a success and that Butch would see again with that eye. I was very happy, even as I marveled again at the ways of God who takes only that He may restore more abundantly. Once I had renounced my own will, He gave me the thing I had most wanted. "My thoughts are not your thoughts, nor My ways, your ways," He said. God help us to think Your thoughts and to walk in Your ways!

On my way home that night, I walked through the rain on sidewalks still covered by ice and snow, but I was not cold. For the first time in days I was so happy that I sang:

> Mary, what a pretty little Baby
> Mary, what a pretty little Baby
> Mary, what a pretty little Baby
> Mary, I give myself unto your Baby
> Mary, I give myself unto your Baby
> Mary, I give myself unto your Baby
> Mary, what a pretty little Baby . . .

I remembered that it was the octave day of the Epiphany. A week ago we had celebrated our birthday with joy. Now there was joy again; but it was a more perfect joy because it was a gift of God.

23

Now, as I finish this, it has been nine months since we moved into the new house. When I started writing, I kept wondering where to end. I thought it would be with the blessing of the new house, but so much has happened since then, that ought to be told. That was not the end, that was just the beginning.

The work keeps growing and so does my own understanding of the problems of the people who are a part of it. Before I opened the house, and even after that, before we moved into the alley, I thought I knew something about poverty. I thought I had been poor. I have never been poor as these people are poor. I never knew about this kind of poverty.

At home, growing up, sometimes the food was not what I wanted, but there was always something nourishing. There was never just rice for breakfast and lunch and supper, as I have seen here. There was space to breathe where we lived. There was a room for parents and a room for children. The boys had their bed, and I had my own.

There were pretty cloths for the tables and clean linens for the bed—and enough of these to go around. There were books to read and a moral code to live by. There was thought and planning and an indefinable spirit that communicated itself from our parents to us, of courage, self-possession, discipline, and love, so that we were not frightened, nor cowed, nor broken by our lack of material things. We had something more important—and we were conscious of it, taking it for granted, unaware of its importance.

Often these people have nothing, or have luxuries without necessities. Or, I might say, looking at the dirty tenements or broken-down shacks in which they must live, and the bare littered yards around them, for them the luxuries have become necessities, because they are the only things that make life bearable, since we have not used the riches and fullness of the material, intellectual or spiritual gifts God has given us as good stewards but have used them selfishly for ourselves, and left these empty.

One day, during a week of house-to-house visiting of the neighborhood with a volunteer, I found a family of a mother and eight children living in one room, with no windows that opened, and two double beds. The room was so small that there were only a few feet between each bed, even though these were against opposite walls. Besides these, there was only room for a box of clothing, a chair, and a table. The room smelled, and the dirty linen on the bed was inadequate to cover the even dirtier mattress. This family had often come to the house for clothing, and the children were always dirty. I had wondered why. Now I saw. The mother was ignorant and given to sloth, in need, and incapable of making a living wage at the only job she knew how to do. Therefore she had given up trying, and lived unashamedly an immoral life, explaining to me, "But I don't let the children know . . . "

Most of these children knew nothing of their fathers. Other people judged her, and people like her, freely, but no one really cared. She drew a welfare check, smaller than her family needs, but the family needed more than money. They needed more than the things money can buy. They needed the personal interest and help of someone who really cared about them. They needed charity in its realest sense.

We found other families like that, though this was the worst.

Then, there was that other poverty we saw in other houses: the poverty of those who have television sets (often not yet paid for in full) and inadequate food, those who have radios and fur coats and shoes with no soles!

At first I was scandalized—then I remembered what my own life had been like, and my own thoughts and ambitions before I loved God. Then things made more sense. I tried to imagine myself, living with others crowded like pigs, in ugly dirty buildings crumbling into ruins, with holes in the ceilings and doors and walls, and nameless musty odors creeping in from under the house and down the halls. I tried to imagine myself growing up listening to the kind of music that blared forth from the radios we passed, and listening every day of my life to the sort of obscenity and filth that passed as commonplace among the neighbors. I tried to imagine myself living in insecurity and fear and ignorance, without the hope of my faith, in a world that despised me because I was poor, and hated me because of my color, and dismissed me because of my ignorance as of no account, and used a machine instead, to do the only work I knew how to perform.

Then I could understand how these could delight in the cheap and tawdry, and raise the sensual to the sublime. I could see why the escape into television, whiskey, and soft, silken fur coats meant more than the dull nourishment of good food, and the feeding of ever-hungry stoves to half heat draughty rooms.

And I knew then that these were my people. Whatever God has given me has not been for myself alone, but for them also. Our Lord belonged to all men, for all time; yet in a very special way it could be said of Him for the Jews, "He came unto His Own, and His Own received Him not." So it is with me. In His Church, He has made me one with all men, bound to love all, destined to share in the glories and the suffering of all, for "we are all one body in Christ." Yet, in a different manner, He has made me one with these, whose blood is like my blood, whose suffering and pain and fear are like my own suffering and pain and fear, springing from the same oppression, whose bitterness is my bitterness and whose shame has been made my shame. In these, my weakness has become magnified and my strength has become stronger.

Yet, paradoxically, even as the house has drawn me closer to my own, it has drawn me closer to others, and not only me, but those others who have been a part of it as volunteers or members of the Outer Circle. There was Jean, whose distrust, suspicion and hate for white people once extended even to white children and to Negroes who spoke well of white people. Now she numbers white people among her friends, and works and plays and talks to white volunteers with ease and unselfconsciousness.

There is Judy, who Father Coyne never thought would remain in the Outer Circle, because it appeared to him that the look of combined contempt, insolence and aversion she cast at the Negro members of the group mirrored prejudiced feeling of such depth that only a miracle could change it. Perhaps it was so. Perhaps the miracle happened, for she has been one of our best friends and most persevering helpers. There has been Alice, who in a Southern white neighborhood has not been ashamed nor afraid to care for a small colored boy, nor ashamed to have him and his mother and their friends as guests in her home, despite raised eyebrows of neighbors. There is Elizabeth, too, and Clark, and Mrs. Cobb and Margaret, who are like her in this.

There is Linda too, who argued about just wages, yet raised her maid's salary without ever saying anything about it to me, because it was not a fair salary. We have helped each other in all needs, material and spiritual. What we had to share, we shared with her; what she had to share, she shared with us—though usually we have been on the receiving end. We have aided her by helping with the house cleaning and baby-sitting, and she has helped us by doing our washing or carrying us about in her car.

There is Bob, who is white, who learned here to diaper colored babies. And Mrs. G., who is colored, who nursed white children because their mother has been a good friend of the house. There are the students from C.B.C., Sienna, Sacred Heart, Holy Names and St. Thomas, whose faith has grown and become practical because in the house they had an opportunity to see how those live who are really poor; and not only to see, but to understand and help.

There is my stepfather, Don, who delights in boasting of his agnosticism; who speaks contemptuously of the

Negro and the poor and who sets up money and "pure" blood streams as blind idols to be served blindly; and who despises half the white race only a degree less than he does the Negro, while he resents and envies most of the other half. He did not want me to open the house. He said that most adults who are destitute deserve no better than they have got. He said, "People are born to be what they are. You can't change them. You can't make runners out of trotters. It takes generations of breeding and selection to change one to another. And generations of people take even longer. But you think you're going down in the rat-holes and make men out of the rats, and women out of the sluts. It can't be done.

"Carrie Nation tried to do it. She was going to close all the saloons, stop whiskey-heads from drinking whiskey and mix the good and bad all up together, thinking 'environment' was going to change men. But a man is born to be what he is. Because of her there were more murders, more racketeers, more whiskey—and poison whiskey at that. The only difference is that the rats, instead of staying in their rat-holes, went into society and politics and big business. That's what happens when you try to mix it all together. Your own Bible tells you 'don't throw your pearls before swine.' It says 'Let Ethom alone.' But *you* are going to take pigs into your living-room and church and schools and try to teach them to be human beings. It won't work. They are going to stay pigs no matter what you do."

(There are a lot of other people I know, too, who share the views he expressed, though they are not usually so blunt and frank in expressing them as he is, nor so free. These others use "nicer" language when they mean the same things. But, back to Don). It was useless to talk to him about grace and love. Despite all of this, and more, he has been a help to the house. When we have had no money, he has given me some, for food for the house, or milk for a baby. He is always coming by the house bringing something for Butch or me, and he always divides with the other children present too. Once, when I was complaining of the seeming density of thought and feeling, and the laziness of a particular person in the house, looking, I suppose, for sympathy from him, or at least for some criticism of the other person, he remarked, surprisingly, "You wanted to share the lives of these people. You say you love them and want to help them. Then this is what you have to take. You just have to bear with her faults, if you're going to have the kind of house you want. She is the cross God has given you to bear."

In my amazement, I was silent. *This* from *him!* There was no sarcasm in his voice, no triumph, no tone that said, "I told you so"; just an amazing gentleness and quiet. "She is the cross God has given." Father Murphy could not have made my duty more clear, nor my shame more complete, nor my contrition more sincere for my lack of charity and humility. Don has learned something from the house, too.

Then there is my father. The house has drawn us closer in a new and stronger love. He encouraged and approved it from the first, because he believes that people are often given little chance to become as good as they might be, especially Negro people. He is glad that there is a place where women of our race in trouble can find love, understanding, and help. And he is glad, too, that these things are not limited to members of our own race if others seek them, but are there for all, for any who will accept what we can give. He has helped us too, with encouragement, with money, and by giving hospitality to children I have taken down for a few days in the country.

There are the children, Butch and Lawrence, who are learning early to give and to share, and to get along with people different in many ways from themselves, in color, in background, in habits. Butch's health has not been injured, as some expected it would be. On the contrary, he is growing stronger. He doesn't wear his brace any more, and he can see with his injured eye, without glasses.

There is Mrs. Cobb, a nurse, a grandmother, and a poet. Long ago, she wanted to do something to help the poor and the colored and she became a nurse. But even this was not enough for her. She wanted to do more. Perhaps it was of this she thought when she wrote in one poem "must spring forever promise, what summer cannot fill?" But now, in the summer of her life, the promise has been fulfilled in her as she works sometimes here as a volunteer, one with us in our poverty and suffering for a few hours.

And there are the others: Denise, who worked with me a year until it became clear that this is not her vocation. But in that year, she who had been far away from God returned to Him and discovered the joy and fullness of Catholic womanhood. She learned what she had never known about obedience, fortitude, and poverty, and because of her, I learned things I needed to know about charity, patience, humility, and meekness. Now she is living at the house, working part-time and going to school full-time. Her teachers commend her for the progress she is making in the profession she is learning.

I only pray that their strength be to do as God wishes *them* to do, and walk the way He wishes *them* to walk.

Often at one or the other church, perhaps at a Third Order meeting, or pontifical Mass to celebrate some anniversary, I meet some of the three or four white members of the study group who, I learned later, left it because they feared I might some day meet them in public and address them by their first names, thus causing them embarrassment before families, friends, or business associates. At the churches they always say "hello" if they see me, even if sometimes a bit hurriedly. I always say "hello" and am careful not to address them by their first names, nor by any name. I will not force them to explain their acquaintance with me nor justify it to their friends, but leave it to their choice and will to know me or not to know me.

Nor can I judge them. God leads different souls by different ways and we all stumble and fall and walk blindly and in darkness until we find His way for us. If they can have peace of conscience in this, I am glad for them, though I cannot understand it. If, as a fault, it calls for God's mercy, I pray for it for them, as I myself need God's mercy to cover and cancel my own faults and sins. If I dared judge anyone intentionally, my own judgment would condemn me to a like punishment. So I pray instead that God's mercy may abound, in order that I also may have a share in it.

And there are still others.

Jim is in the army now. He was home after he left the seminary only a few months before he went into the service. I don't know in what ways the house has influenced him, but in this: he has been able to see put into practice what were many of our intellectual convictions, and has come to admit that human prudence is not the same as supernatural prudence, that "the wisdom of men is foolishness with God."

Rosemary and Morris are happy in their new home in Chicago with their family. They are glad that their children will not have to grow up under the handicap of a segregated second-class citizenship. They do not want to come back here to live. But their oldest child, my godchild, is still here. She lived with me at Blessed Martin House for a while and was a big help to me. Now she has a family of her own, though. Still, I see her every once in a while. She comes by to show me her baby, a pretty little boy.

Joan, Jane, and the girl scouts are all living out of town now too, but we hear of Joan now and then, and once or twice she has been by the House.

Charlene has made her profession and is now a sister in Baltimore.

The Smiths still help occasionally with a plumbing problem, and Mr. Childs, who is very sick these days, still helps with his prayers and the offerings of his suffering and blindness.

Elizabeth and Clark, Dan and Alice, Eugenia and Fred all have had several additions to their families in the last years, so they haven't been able to come down often, as they used to do. Each family has six children, and that is quite a job in itself. However, all these still help by offering hospitality to guests at the house, driving us places we want to go—sewing, typing, telephoning, propaganda, all things which they can do in their own homes.

Some of the younger members of the group of the Outer Circle also help in these ways. In fact, some of this book was typed by volunteers such as these. For the younger group, however, there is still much opposition from families who cannot understand.

Only recently the mother of one such volunteer called me again to tell me that she was returning to me some material which I had given her daughter to type for me. She asked me not to call her daughter any more, nor ask her to help me in any way.

"Do your work yourself," she commanded me, with a certain grimness. She is a good woman, and deeply fervent in her own way. But ours is a way she cannot understand. She fears it and wants to safeguard her family from it. To her, it is *my* work.

What can I say to the volunteers placed in this position? I cannot say, "You should do this," or "You should do that." I do not know. I can understand that they do not want to help me surreptitiously, as if it were a crime. Nor do they want to help openly if it will mean serious discord in their familes, as it certainly will. The Spirit breathes where He wills and God leads each soul by its own way. On one hand He says, "Honor your father and your mother," and on the other, He says, "He that loveth father and mother more than Me is not worthy of Me," and "If any man come to me and hate not his father and mother and wife and children . . . yea and his own life also, he cannot be my disciple." The Christian way is between two extremes, and each soul must find its own way. Our thoughts are not the thoughts of God, nor are our ways His ways, for "My thoughts are not your thoughts: nor your ways My ways, saith the Lord. For as the heavens are exalted above the earth, so are My ways exalted above your ways, and My thoughts above your thoughts."

Does that mean, then, that we have gone as far as we are going, and that now we can rest complacently in the thought of the good God has already been pleased to work through us and permit us to see? Of course not. We are only infants, we haven't even learned to walk or stand yet, but creep about, stumbling, making the same mistakes over and over, until our Mother pities us and takes us in her arms, soothing us and carrying us about until we are stronger, until our Father gives us more of His strength.

268

We are only begining, or perhaps only getting ready to begin.

Yesterday Our Lord taught us a little about charity through a woman who was poor and sick and mean and lazy and ungrateful.

Today He teaches us about poverty by taking from us the things we thought we needed and giving us only what He knows we really need. Once I thought we had to have a telephone, but we could no longer pay for it, so the company took it away. I find we got along very well without it; only then did we get it back. All in the house have learned that we can enjoy food we once thought we did not like and could not eat, when it is given to us, because that is what we have. It is the feast God Himself has prepared for us, and how can we not enjoy it and be grateful? Dorothy Day often speaks of the precariousness of poverty. That is the hardest thing to bear about poverty, and it is this we want to share and do share.

Tomorrow, when we have learned this lesson well, when we have learned how utterly we are dependent on Him, not only for our existence but for our sustenance as well, then He will teach us something else. Maybe it will be suffering, borne joyfully and with meekness. Maybe He will teach us patience, that we may wait His time for all things in serenity and peace. Maybe He will teach us something of silence in order that we may speak only what is good and true and useful, and often refrain from speaking at all, in order that we may hear the voice of Our Lord speaking in us in our soul's silence.

It does not matter; it is in His hands. We go where He leads us with joy and contentment. The worst has already happened: sin has come into the world, and we were a part of it. But the damage has already been repaired, the fault has already been forgiven, for God has come into the world. The Word was made Flesh. God became man, that men might share in the life of God; God has loved us and enabled us to love Him in return, and love each other in Him for His sake.

Why then should we be afraid of suffering, of poverty, of insecurity and humiliations? Why should we fear oppression, failure, or any other adversity? God is. He loves us. He died that we might live with Him forever in the happiness of Heaven. All that we need to do is use the grace He gives us. And grace is free.